POCKET
DICTIONARY *of*
NORTH AMERICAN
DENOMINATIONS

EDITED BY DREW BLANKMAN
& TODD AUGUSTINE

InterVarsity Press
Downers Grove, Illinois

Preface

Denominations have been part of the Christian landscape since the Reformation. That seismic shift gave us the Lutherans and the Reformed and the Anabaptist Brethren and Mennonites. (Of course, the Catholics and the Orthodox already had been around for hundreds of years before that.) Under Henry VIII, the Church of England declared its independence from the Church of Rome, and from within the Anglican communion emerged Congregationalists and Baptists and Presbyterians and Quakers and Methodists, as well as other independent and nonconformist groups.

North America not only inherited this denominational diversity but fostered even more. So new formations emerged, including Disciples and Pentecostals and Bible Churches and Mormons and Free Churches and independent megachurches. How are we to keep track of all these groups, our neighbors, that claim to be part of (or to even be *the*) body of Christ?

The award-winning *Dictionary of Christianity in America (DCA)*, which was released in 1990, has a wealth of information about people, events, theology, movements and, yes, denominations. Unfortunately, the *DCA* has been out of print for a number of years now. The *Pocket Dictionary of North American Denominations*, based on articles culled from the *DCA*, gives new life to an important slice of its resources.

Much has changed since the *DCA* was published—for example, the Evangelical Lutheran Church of America was formed through the merger of three Lutheran denominations, the Worldwide Church of God morphed from an unorthodox sect to an evangelical denomination, and Willow Creek Community Church spawned the Willow Creek Association—so the *DCA* articles used in this dictionary have been edited and updated. Thus any inaccuracies should not be attributed to the original contributors and editors but to the present editors.

There are thousands of denominations in North America. In a reference book of this size, there is no way we could include all of them.

However, we have included most of the major denominations and associations as well as some smaller movements and groups. In this dictionary you will find listed alphabetically more than one hundred Orthodox, Catholic and Protestant groups, and a few others that are considered unorthodox by most Christians. Within an article an asterisk (*) in front of a group's name means that there is an article on that group in this dictionary.

Though the articles in this *Pocket Dictionary* supply you with key historical dates, important distinctives and the basic theology of each denomination, they just begin to scratch the surface. We have also attempted to give you the most up-to-date membership statistics. However, accurate information is notoriously difficult or even impossible to access for some groups. For more information regarding North American denominations and religious movements we suggest you refer to Frank S. Mead's *Handbook of Denominations in the United States* (11th ed.), Arthur Piepkorn's *Profiles in Belief* or visit the denominations' websites, which usually include their history, fundamental beliefs and organizational structure. At the end of each article you will usually find the denomination's address, phone and fax numbers, and Internet home page. Some groups, however, do not disseminate such information or are not yet on the Web.

The Editors

A

African Methodist Episcopal Church. The largest African American Methodist denomination. The African Methodist Episcopal Church (AMEC) was founded by Richard Allen and his followers, who refused to accept their second-class status in St. George's Methodist Episcopal Church in Philadelphia. At Sunday services in November 1787, the trustees of St. George's tried to remove the African American members from their places of prayer at the altar. Allen and Absalom Jones led the African American members of the congregation out of the church in protest. With his own money, Allen purchased a blacksmith shop and began holding services there, eventually naming it Bethel.

African American members of two white churches in Baltimore also declared their independence and established the Colored Methodist Society. In 1801 Daniel Coker became the leader of the Baltimore group, which also named their church Bethel. In April 1816 representatives from the Bethel churches in Philadelphia and Baltimore, and African American Methodists from other communities, met at Bethel Church in Philadelphia to establish the AMEC. Bishop Francis Asbury of the Methodist Episcopal Church (*see* United Methodist Church) consecrated Allen as the first bishop of the church. The AMEC Discipline, Twenty-five Articles of Religion, General Rules and the episcopal structure remained close in doctrine and practice to the Methodist Episcopal Church.

The church began the AME Book Concern, the first publishing house owned and operated by African Americans. In 1847 the church began publishing a weekly magazine, which became *The Christian Recorder*, the oldest African American newspaper in the world. The first AME college, Wilberforce University, was founded in 1856. In 1883 they began the *AME Church Review*, the oldest African American magazine published by African Americans.

The AMEC expanded from 20,000 members in 1856 to over 200,000 members by 1876. The church established foreign missions to the Caribbean, South America and Africa. Before the Civil War, the church had fulfilled a strongly felt obligation to Africa with missionaries like Daniel Coker, who went to Liberia in 1820 under the auspices of the American Colonization Society, and Scipio Bean, who went to Haiti in 1827. After the Civil War, Bishop Henry Mc-

Neal Turner and Martin Delaney continued to advocate a religious pan-Africanism and black nationalism.

The denomination has thirteen districts with thirteen bishops. The last statistics provided in 2000 showed that there were 6,000 churches with a membership of 2,311,398 in the U.S. There are nine AMEC congregations in Canada.

3801 Market St., Suite 300
Philadelphia, PA 29204
Phone: (215) 662-0506
Website: www.amecnet.org

African Methodist Episcopal Zion Church. Second-largest African American Methodist denomination. In 1796 several men led disaffected African American members out of John's Street Methodist Episcopal Zion Church in New York, refusing to accept the discrimination and segregation imposed by the church. James Varick and other African American leaders petitioned Bishop Francis Asbury to let them hold their own meetings apart from the John's Street Church. Bishop Asbury approved the request and separate meetings began in 1796, and the first church, called Zion, was built in 1800. A year later, the church received its charter under the name *African Methodist Episcopal Church of the City of New York.*

Until he left the Methodist Episcopal Church in 1820, a white member of the John's Street Church, William Stillwell, served as minister for both congregations. When Zion church members could find no one in the Episcopal or the Methodist churches to ordain or consecrate their elders, they consecrated them independently. At the first annual conference held on June 21, 1821, nineteen preachers representing six African American Methodist churches in New York, New Haven, Newark and Philadelphia organized the African Methodist Episcopal Zion Church (AMEZC) with Varick as the first bishop. The AMEZC adopted the rituals and doctrines of the Methodist Episcopal Church as found in the Twenty-five Articles of Religion, the Discipline, the General Rules and the episcopal structure. The denomination's episcopal polity divides the church into twelve districts with twelve bishops. The name *African Methodist Episcopal Zion Church* was adopted in 1848.

After the Civil War, the AMEZ churches spread throughout the

South. Home missions were established in Louisiana, Mississippi and Oklahoma. By 1880 the church not only had fifteen annual conferences in the South, but in that same year it established Livingstone College at Salisbury, North Carolina, the church's largest educational institution. Eventually the church founded five secondary schools and two colleges, including Hood Theological Seminary.

In 1906 the denomination had 184,542 members in 2,197 churches in the U.S. In 1999 the AMEZ Church reported approximately 2,500,000 members in 6,200 churches.

3225 West Sugar Creek Rd.
Charlotte, NC 28269
Phone: (704) 599-4630; Fax (704) 688-2549

Amana Church Society. Pietist sect previously known as the Community of True Inspiration. Formed in Hesse, Germany, in 1714 by Johann Friedrich Rock and Eberhardt Ludwig Gruber, these "new prophets" taught that the age of true and direct divine inspiration (with authority equal to Scripture) had not ended. The inspired community lived simply, practiced nonresistance and held love feasts much like other radical Pietists. Although they expanded in areas of toleration, a period of quietism and spiritual decline set in after the death of Rock in 1749.

The movement was renewed during the early nineteenth century through two new inspired leaders, Barbara Heinmann (later Landmann) and Christian Metz. Inhospitable conditions, however, led to their immigration to New York in 1842. There they established the village of Ebenezer, near Buffalo, and were reorganized into a communal society. Between 1855 and 1864 the Inspirationists moved from corrupting urban influences to a large tract near Iowa City, Iowa. Seven prosperous villages, collectively known as the Amana colonies (*Amana* means "remain faithful") were eventually established. Membership in the society reached its peak of 1,813 in 1880.

In 1932 internal dissension and external pressures led to a dissolution of communal ties and the creation of an independent church society. The assets of the community were divided and a joint stock company created in which the members received shares. Worship is conducted in seven congregations with a total of approximately 500 members by the society's elders and includes reading testimonies from previous inspired prophets, the last of whom died in 1883.

Attn: Church Administrator
Middle Amana, IA 52307

American Baptist Association. A Landmark Baptist organization. The formation of the American Baptist Association in Arkansas in 1905 was the culmination of the struggle of Landmarkism in the Southern Baptist Convention (SBC). In the 1850s Landmarkism, under the leadership of J. R. Graves, advocated an ecclesiology that emphasized the local church. Tenets included (1) Baptist churches are the only true churches, (2) the true church is a local visible institution, (3) the churches and the kingdom of God are coterminous, (4) valid ordination derives from a Baptist church, (5) only valid ministers can administer the Lord's Supper and baptism, (6) Baptist churches have an unbroken historical succession back to the New Testament, (7) and missionary work is to be done by local churches rather than convention boards.

In 1899 Landmarkers formed their first state organization, the East Texas Baptist Convention, later known by the name the *Baptist Missionary Association* (BMA). With Samuel A. Hayden as its most prominent leader, the BMA was outspoken against the SBC and its method of carrying out missionary work through a convention rather than through local churches.

In 1902 Arkansas's "anticonvention" forces rallied against the state convention and formed the General Association of Arkansas Baptists. Under the dynamic leadership of Ben M. Bogard, an attempt was made in 1905 to convert the SBC to Landmark views regarding mission methods. Although the attempt failed, Bogard's movement absorbed smaller Landmark bodies, including the BMA of Texas, and was renamed the *American Baptist Association* in 1924. With headquarters in Texarkana, Arkansas, the ABA operates several schools, a seminary in Little Rock and a publishing house. In the late 1990s there were over 1,760 affiliated churches and an inclusive membership of approximately 250,000.

4605 N. State Line Ave.
Texarkana, TX 75503
Phone: (903) 792-2783
Website: www.abaptist.com

American Baptist Churches in the U.S.A. A major Baptist denomination, formerly known as the American Baptist Convention (1950-1972) and the Northern Baptist Convention (1907-1950). On May 17, 1907, delegates from local churches, Baptist state conventions and city mission societies of the Northern U.S., leaders of the American Baptist Foreign and Home Mission Societies plus the American Baptist Publication Society, met at Calvary Baptist Church in Washington, D.C., to organize formally the Northern Baptist Convention, a loosely federated body of churches and benevolent organizations dedicated to "better and more coherent action as a purely advisory body."

From the establishment of the first Baptist congregation in America at Providence, Rhode Island, around 1638, Baptists cherished the local governance of their churches. Even with the creation of the first regional association of churches in New England in 1670 (General Six Principle Baptists) and Philadelphia in 1707 (Philadelphia Baptist Association), each local congregation was said to have complete power and authority from Jesus Christ. Gradually, in the second half of the eighteenth century, Baptists grew in numbers and sought to cooperate in evangelism, missions and educational enterprises. Permanent organizations beyond local churches evolved slowly. In general, associations gathered as confessional bodies of fellowship and mutual support, and to review and debate matters of concern.

Beginning in 1802 Baptists in New England organized a series of benevolent societies to advance the denominational interests. Until 1845, when the Southern Baptist Convention was formed, these societies represented congregations in the South and West as well. An organizational principle of voluntary individual membership with independent charters dominated Baptist life in the Northern states throughout the nineteenth century. This was in marked contrast to the more centralized convention model that Baptists in the Southern states created in 1845.

The driving impulse of Baptists in the North from 1814 was foreign missions. The first national body was organized that year as the General Baptist Missionary Convention, which soon grew to include a college, a seminary and domestic mission endeavors. In 1824 the Baptist General Tract Society was organized (later the American

Baptist Publication and Sunday School Society), and in 1832 the American Baptist Home Mission Society started in New York City. Women's missionary societies were chartered in the 1870s, and separate conferences for ethnically and racially diverse peoples emerged, beginning in 1851, for German, Swedish, Danish-Norwegian, Italian and Hispanic Americans. Sometimes overlapping in programs, often competing in stewardship drives, the Baptist society model in the North was focused sharply on the local churches, which jealously guarded their autonomy. When financial exigency threatened around 1900, interagency agreements and planning meetings eventually led to the creation of a unified Northern Baptist Convention (NBC) in 1905.

In 1911 a merger was effected with the Free Baptist General Conference, the organization of the Freewill Baptists in America. Structurally, Northern Baptists created boards for ministerial pensions and education and several commissions for stewardship, missions and social service. Controversy ensued over these rapid advances, and the Convention delegates found themselves embroiled in self-destructive debates by 1920 between the modernists and fundamentalists. Clusters of churches in the Northeast, Ohio Valley and Oregon bolted the Convention and organized new theologically conservative associations which prevented binding legislative action beyond the local congregations. The main body of Northern Baptists in 1922 assumed a mediating position, affirming the New Testament as the "all sufficient ground of faith and practice."

Delegates to the 1950 annual meeting of the convention voted to change the name to American Baptist Convention (ABC) and an open invitation was given to other Baptist bodies to unite with the ABC and achieve a national Baptist body. While many congregations in the African American Baptist traditions achieved a dual-alignment status and the Convention negotiated an associated relationship with the Church of the Brethren, no organic union took place. Instead, American Baptists have participated in more collegial efforts such as the Baptist World Alliance and the Baptist Jubilee Advance in 1964.

In 1972 a major revision of American Baptist denominational structures was adopted and a new, more connectional polity resulted in the American Baptist Churches in the U.S.A. (ABC-USA).

A greater share of authority was given to the regional bodies and local churches, with policy matters being ratified by a more democratic general board, composed of clergy and laity. A series of "covenants of relationships" unites the interests, tasks and resources of sixty distinct regional, national and general organizations.

As of 2001, the ABC-USA claimed 5,786 churches and 1,442,824 members in all fifty states. About 800 congregations were dually aligned with one or more of the African American Baptist or mainline Protestant groups. Of the 8,856 ordained clergy the ABC-USA recognized, 434 were women. Theologically, American Baptists are broadly evangelical, with churches and pastors representing conservative, neo-orthodox and liberal traditions.

Denominational interests are coordinated at the national offices in Valley Forge, Pennsylvania, and at thirty-seven regional, state and city locations across the U.S. Churches in a region or state generally meet annually in conventions, while elected convention delegates, representatives to the General Board and program administrators hold a Biennial Meeting in various cities throughout the U.S. and Puerto Rico. There are fifteen colleges or universities, six theological schools, and 122 homes, children's centers and hospitals affiliated with the denomination. The official periodical, *The American Baptist*, is said to be the oldest Christian magazine continuously in print in North America.

P.O. Box 851
Valley Forge, PA 19482-0851
Phone: (800) ABC-3USA
Website: www.abc-usa.org

American Lutheran Church. *See* Evangelical Lutheran Church in America.

Amish, Old Order. One of several North American groups whose roots go back to the sixteenth-century Swiss Anabaptists. During the years 1693-1697 the Swiss Brethren (today called Mennonites) experienced a schism. The one faction, led by Jakob Ammann, decided to reject the new spirit of Pietism that was influencing many Swiss Mennonites and introduced some Dutch Mennonite elements, as found in the Dutch Dordrecht Confession of 1632. These included the ordinance of foot washing and a strict approach to the *Meidung* (shunning, or the avoidance of excommunicated persons). Ammann believed men should wear untrimmed beards and promoted a modest attire.

Various Swiss Mennonite congregations decided in favor of Jakob Ammann's views; some resided in Switzerland and others in Alsace and the Palatinate, where Swiss Mennonites had relocated for economic and political reasons. Sometime after 1710 Amish families began immigrating to North America, so that by 1787 some seventy congregations were established in Pennsylvania. Soon thereafter the Amish joined in the general westward movement into Ohio, Indiana and elsewhere.

From 1862 to 1878 the Amish entered into formal conference discussions that led to a schism. One group decided for the "Old Order"; the other accepted more progressive ideas. Most congregations in the latter group, called Amish-Mennonites, eventually merged with the *Mennonite Church. Today the Old Order Amish live in several states and the province of Ontario, with their largest concentrations in Ohio (Holmes County), Pennsylvania (Lancaster County) and northern Indiana. Currently there are approximately 145,000 Amish men, women and children living in twenty-two states in the United States and in Ontario, Canada.

National Committee for Amish Religious Freedom
30650 Six Mile Road
Livonia, MI 48154
Phone: (734) 427-1414

Anglican Church of Canada. Although the first Anglican worship service on Canadian soil was conducted by Robert Wolfall at Frobisher Bay, Baffin Island, on September 2, 1578, it was over two centuries before the first bishop was appointed. In the meantime, the young British colonies in eastern Canada were ministered to by naval or military chaplains or by missionaries sent from England by the Society for the Propagation of the Gospel in Foreign Parts (SPG).

The Irish-born Loyalist Charles Inglis became the first Anglican bishop in Canada, then British North America (BNA) in 1787. Based in Halifax, he had episcopal oversight of all BNA colonies.

In 1856 Bishop John Strachan of Toronto convened the first diocesan synod in the history of the Church of England and, in the following year, Benjamin Cronyn of Huron became the first bishop to be elected to office by a synod. In 1860 Bishop Francis Fulford was elected as the first Metropolitan of the self-governing Ecclesiastical Province of Canada. Apart from British Columbia, the other dioceses in Western Canada formed themselves into the Province of Rupert's Land in 1875. Its first Metropolitan, Archbishop Robert Machray, was elected Primate of All Canada at the inaugural General Synod of the Church of England in Canada in September 1893. There are now thirty dioceses grouped into four Ecclesiastical Provinces. In 1999, the Anglican Church of Canada (as it was called after 1955) claimed approximately 686,000 members (3.4 percent of the Canadian population).

In the twentieth century, the Anglican Church of Canada inaugurated many liberalizing policies involving significant changes in structure, theology and outlook, which have given rise to the ordination of women to the priesthood, liturgical revision (including the recent publication of the *Book of Alternative Services*), the peace movement, the use of inclusive language, homosexual rights and support for native land claims. However, since each diocese is autonomous in its government, there are differences across the country in the extent to which such policies have been adopted

600 Jarvis Street
Toronto, Ontario M4Y 2J6
Phone: (416) 924-9192
Website: www.anglican.ca

Armenian Church. A non-Chalcedonian Orthodox church. Christianity in Armenia dates at least from the third century and was proclaimed the official state religion in 301, making Armenia the first Christian nation.

The Armenian Church belongs to the family of Eastern Orthodox churches commonly referred to as Oriental, or Non-Chalcedonian, Orthodox churches because of their opposition to the Council of Chalcedon (451) and advocacy of the Christological doctrine of St. Cyril of Alexandria. The Oriental Orthodox churches adhere to the doctrinal decrees of the Councils of Nicea (325), Constantinople (381) and Ephesus (431).

Very few Armenians arrived on the shores of the U.S. until the first half of the nineteenth century. Armenian immigrants from the Ottoman Empire came to the U.S. during the last quarter of the nineteenth century, many planning to make their fortunes and return to their homeland. But political instability in Armenia kept them in America. By 1888 there were approximately twelve hundred Armenians in the U.S., concentrated mostly around New York City; Providence, Rhode Island; Boston and Worcester, Massachusetts; and Fresno, California.

To minister to the spiritual needs of the growing community, the Rev. Hovsep Sarajian arrived in the U.S. from Constantinople in 1889 and celebrated the first Divine Liturgy in Worcester, Massachusetts, on July 28 of that same year. The first Armenian church was consecrated in Worcester on January 18, 1891. As the flow of immigrants continued and as the community grew, so did the number of parishes. New churches were consecrated in Fresno, California (1900); West Hoboken, New Jersey (1907); and Fowler, California (1910).

Catholicos Mugurditch I (1892-1907) gave permanence to the presence of the Armenian Church in America when his encyclical of 1898 formally established the Diocese of the Armenian Church of America. The Rev. Hovsep Sarajian was its first primate. At the turn of the century the Armenian community in the U.S. numbered over 15,000, with four established churches and six priests. The community grew further during the first two decades of the twentieth century. Toward the end of the 1920s, there were nineteen churches in the U.S. and over thirty-five parishes, in various stages of formation, served by more than thirty priests.

Internal conflict within the community in 1933 led to the establishment of a rival diocesan jurisdiction. The schism remains unresolved to this day. The next decades brought further growth to the church. In the early 1960s the St. Nersess Theological Seminary was established.

Beginning in the early 1970s, a major and ongoing wave of new immigrants from various Middle Eastern countries has brought the number of Armenians in the U.S. to an estimated population of over 750,000, making it the largest Armenian population in any country outside Armenia. In 1984 the Diocese of Canada was established, which was part of the Eastern Diocese of the U.S. Presently there are over one hundred churches and mission parishes in the U.S., divided into two jurisdictions: the Eastern Diocese with its headquarters in New York City, and the Western Diocese centered in Los Angeles. Since 1959 the Armenian Church has been a member of the National Council of Churches.

The Diocese of the Armenian Church of America (Eastern)
630 Second Avenue
New York, NY 10016
Website: www.armenianchurch.org

Assemblies of God. Pentecostal denomination. Formed in April 1914 in Hot Springs, Arkansas, the Assemblies of God (AG), with well over 15 million adherents, is today the largest Pentecostal denomination in the world. The denomination began inauspiciously when some 300 believers responded to a call to a convention at Hot Springs. Approximately 120 of them were delegates from scattered Pentecostal ministries who shared concerns about their movement's future. While they nurtured an intense dislike for established denominations, they concluded that limited cooperation would be in their best interests and created the General Council of the Assemblies of God. Refusing to adopt a statement of faith, they did agree to encourage support for foreign missions and Bible institute education and to issue credentials to would-be workers who met certain qualifications. They also stated their intention to disapprove theological and practical "error."

Their sense of participation in a broader religious awakening was nurtured by a wide variety of Pentecostal periodicals and frequent camp meetings and conventions. Otherwise, they worked independently, with a strong stress on the restoration of New Testament Christianity, evangelism, healing and the imminence of the Second Coming. They reveled in intense religious experiences; for them Pentecostalism was a way of life, a way of perceiving reality.

Their reluctance to adopt a creed was challenged by the emergence of unorthodox trinitarian views within the constituency. In 1916 the fledgling denomination adopted a Statement of Fundamental Truths, which addressed the trinitarian question and defined a Pentecostal distinctive but omitted such doctrines as the virgin birth. In 1918 the AG moved its headquarters to Springfield, Missouri, where it is housed today in a multimillion-dollar complex. In 1962, as the denomination became more thoroughly evangelical and asserted its evangelical identity more formally, statements on the verbal inspiration of Scripture, the virgin birth and other doctrines affirmed in the National Association of Evangelicals' statement of faith were added to the Statement of Fundamental Truths.

Those who formed the AG had anticipated that believers should experience one work of grace, not two (as their Holiness counterparts urged), and the baptism with the Holy Spirit. Over the years, however, views on progressive sanctification and the Trinity have most clearly defined the differences between the Assemblies of God and several other predominantly white Pentecostal groups. In 1918 the denomination excluded some who questioned its view of evidential tongues. The trend toward conformity was reinforced. In four years it had become evident that, rhetoric aside, the Assemblies of God was a denomination rather than the loosely structured fellowship it claimed to be. When it adopted a constitution in 1927, the formal process was complete.

From the outset the denomination supported a growing missions program. By the mid-1980s the Assemblies of God annually devoted some $135 million (nearly 75 percent of its total expenditures) to its various world ministries, in which some 1,500 missionaries served in 118 countries. More than 250 Bible institutes abroad train nationals; the denomination's radio program, "Revivaltime," is aired in over 100 countries. Home missions efforts started more slowly, but since 1937 they have targeted various ethnic and handicapped constituencies in North America.

In 1922 the denomination opened Central Bible Institute (now Central Bible College) in Springfield, Missouri, primarily conceived to offer practical training for Pentecostal pastors, evangelists and missionaries. Other schools were sponsored by local districts. In the mid-1980s, the denomination's fifty-seven districts sponsored thirteen colleges and several nonaccredited institutes. In 1955 the Assemblies of God opened Evangel College, a four-year liberal arts institution in Springfield, Missouri. In 1973 the AG opened a theological seminary at the denomination's headquarters in Springfield. A denomination that had once disavowed formal training except at the institute level (with a practical rather than a reflective emphasis) had discovered a commitment to Christian education that now extends to local-church-sponsored elementary and high schools as well.

Since the mid-1970s the AG has been cited in several years as the fastest-growing American denomination. Although congregations average about 115 members, the denomination has numerous congregations with membership in the thousands.

The AG, despite strong centralizing tendencies, continues to assert the primacy of the local congregation. Congregations are organized into districts, and districts ordain and discipline ministers. Each district is governed by a district council, which has its own superintendent and presbytery. All fifty-seven district superintendents, plus two elected representatives from each district, compose the denomination's general presbytery, which meets annually. Every two years all ordained and licensed ministers meet in General Council sessions. The General Council governs the denomination through thirteen elected executives.

Doctrinally, the AG has become more precise since 1914. Efforts to discourage dissent have resulted in strong affirmations of both premillennialism and the denomination's distinctive doctrine of tongues as uniform initial evidence of Spirit baptism. Growth and problems have stimulated centralization and organization. Upward mobility and higher education have challenged assumptions of an earlier era when Pentecostalism was less an intellectual persuasion and more a way of experiencing and interpreting reality.

A large and growing denomination, the Assemblies of God perceives itself as an evangelical denomination (it associated with the National Association of Evangelicals in the early 1940s) with a difference. But the difference is increasingly obscured by religious and cultural change. As of 2001, there were 12,082 churches with an inclusive membership of 2,627,029.

General Council of the Assemblies of God
1445 Boonville Avenue
Springfield, MO 65802
Phone: (417) 862-2781; Fax: (417) 862-8558
Website: www.ag.org

Associate Reformed Presbyterian Church. *See* General Synod of the Associate Reformed Presbyterian Church.

Associated Gospel Churches. A Canadian evangelical denomination, and one of the few Christian bodies indigenous to Canada. The roots of the Associated Gospel Churches (AGC) lay in the intense evangelistic/revivalistic and missionary movement of the late nineteenth century. Its founders, fearing the rise of nonevangelical views of theology and the Christian life, found meaning in premillennialism, with its pessimistic understanding of the future of the church and society in this age. Moving in the orbit of fundamentalism, with its generally Calvinistic orientation, AGC laid great stress on the eternal security of the believer.

The key figure in the formation of the AGC was Peter W. Philpott, a one-time Brigadier of the Salvation Army. From 1896 to 1922 he ministered in Hamilton, Ontario, where he established the downtown Gospel Tabernacle, which soon was filled with 1,600 people. Satellite congregations were also founded.

In order to provide mutual encouragement, a few of these congregations came together in 1921 to form the AGC. In 1922 Philpott left for the pastorate of the Moody Church, Chicago, and later the Church of the Open Door, Los Angeles. With its leader gone, and the group facing a somewhat different era, the new denomination slowly developed. It has now grown to a membership of some 10,000 in 135 congregations across Canada, more than half of which are in southern Ontario.

3228 South Service Road
Burlington, ON L7H 3H8
Phone: (905) 634-8184; Fax: (905) 634-6283
Website: www.agcofcanada.com

Association of Vineyard Churches. A new evangelical denomination emphasizing charismatic gifts of the Holy Spirit. In 1974 Kenn and Joanie Gulliksen were sent out from Calvary Chapel, Costa Mesa, to plant another Chapel in the Los Angeles area. After successfully planting several churches, the Gulliksen's renamed them The Vineyard. At about the same time, Carol Wimber, wife of John Wimber (a former pop musician and a copastor of a *Friends church) started a home Bible study along with some of the leaders of her church. In a few months the group grew to about 100, and John became its leader. In 1977 the Wimbers' study group became part of the Calvary Chapel movement. John Wimber and Kenn Gulliksen first met in 1979, and in 1982 Wimber's Calvary Chapel of Yorba Linda joined the Vineyard movement. Wimber soon became the head of the Vineyard, and in 1985 he, in association with other Vineyard leaders, incorporated the Association of Vineyard Churches (AVC).

Vineyard churches are evangelical and orthodox in their doctrine. However, they differ from other evangelical churches in that they believe that evangelism and the advancement of the kingdom of God requires visible demonstrations of the power of God over the kingdom of darkness (led by Satan and his demonic hosts). Thus after biblical exposition, Vineyard worship emphasizes the public display of the supernatural gifts of the Holy Spirit. In addition, Vineyard worship is known for its contemporary praise songs, many of which are used in non-Vineyard churches throughout the U.S.

In the U.S. each of the AVC's eight regions comprise clusters of churches overseen by an Area Pastor Coordinator (APC). The APCs are in turn led by a Regional Overseer. The National Director guides the Regional Overseers. In the early 2000s the Vineyard had 850 churches, 500 of which are in the U.S., with over 100,000 members.

P.O. Box 2089
Stafford, TX 77497-8461
Phone. (201) 313-0463, Fax. (201) 313-0464
Website: www.vineyardusa.org

B

Baptist General Conference. A Baptist denomination. The Baptist General Conference originated in the great evangelical revival of the nineteenth century. Its specific roots were Swedish Pietism. Simple biblical faith, dedicated evangelism, rejection of formalism and a demand for a regenerate clergy were the trademarks of the Baptists in the Scandinavian homeland.

The first Swedish Baptist congregation in America was founded in 1852 at Rock Island, Illinois, by Anders Wiberg and Gustaf Palmquist. By 1871 the Swedish Baptists had grown to 1,500 members in congregations dispersed over seven states. The church grew with the influx of Swedish immigrants in the late nineteenth century, and by 1902 there were 22,000 members in 324 churches. A Canadian branch was established at Winnipeg in 1894.

The national body became known as the Swedish Baptist General Conference in 1879. Prior to World War II the Conference maintained its ethnic identity, though English gradually replaced Swedish in worship services. In 1945 the Conference, by then numbering 40,000 adherents and more comfortable with its American identity, dropped *Swedish* from its title.

The Conference operates Bethel Seminary and Bethel College in St. Paul, Minnesota, originally founded in Chicago during the late nineteenth century by pastor John Alexis Edgren. The college, established as a four-year liberal arts college in 1947, began as a Bible and missionary school in 1922. The Conference operates a foreign missions program reaching Asia, Africa and Latin America. In 2002 there were 193,160 members in 902 churches.

2002 S. Arlington Heights Rd.
Arlington Heights, IL 60005
Phone: (847) 228-0200; Fax: (847) 228-5376
Website: www.bgcworld.org

Baptist Union of Western Canada. *See* Canadian Baptist Ministries.

Bible Church Movement. The name generally applied to the hundreds of denominationally unaffiliated churches which developed primarily in the U.S. during the twentieth century. Although some Bible churches have no affiliation with any group, many are in fellowship with organizations such as the Independent Fundamental Churches of America, the American Council of Christian Churches and the National Association of Evangelicals.

The movement has its roots in Great Britain in the teaching of John Nelson Darby (1800-1882) and his followers, who rejected the concept of a state church and urged believers to deny the legitimacy of all denominations. Darby's view of the church emphasized the apostate nature of Christendom and argued for total separation from existing denominational structures. Darby viewed the true church as temporary, established by God to cover the dispensation of grace from the cross to the second coming. He believed that denominationalism is wrong because it appeals to the outward profession, whereas the true church consists of the inward "unity of the Spirit." The movement received further support from the revivalistic efforts of D. L. Moody and his successors, who resisted denominationalism and led cooperative, interchurch campaigns, appealing for support to all evangelical denominations. Moody's Chicago Avenue Church was one of the earliest nondenominational ministries in the U.S.

Darby made six trips to the U.S. and Canada between 1859 and 1874. He visited most of the major cities and spoke in many pulpits of prominent American churchmen, particularly those who embraced premillennialism. Darby's eschatological views were widely accepted by American pastors and teachers, but his ecclesiology was not endorsed by most American churchmen during his lifetime. When the modernist-fundamentalist conflicts arose in the denominations during the late nineteenth and early twentieth centuries, many then accepted Darby's views on apostasy and separated from their denominations, although most did not join the *Plymouth Brethren movement, which he had helped found.

Bible churches emphasize biblical preaching. This often means expository preaching. The attempt is made to compare Scripture with Scripture in an effort to determine all that the Bible has to say about a particular subject or theme. Members typically follow closely the preaching and teaching centered on the text.

Bible churches receive their support entirely from the freewill offerings of the members. They emphasize tithing by the members, and some refuse to pass an offering plate because that might entice a nonbeliever to contribute to the work of the church. They typically emphasize individual conversion, interpret the Scriptures in a literal manner and advocate a strict separation from the world in personal conduct. They stress evangelism, although they often have a strong disposition against collaboration with city-wide campaigns that include ecumenical representations. They contribute generously to the support of interdenominational home and foreign missions, particularly the faith missions.

Brethren in Christ Church. A small American denomination with Anabaptist, pietistic and Wesleyan Holiness roots. The Brethren in Christ emerged from the pietistic revival movements in Lancaster County, Pennsylvania, during the latter years of the eighteenth century. The founders (among them Jacob Engel), largely Anabaptist in background, experienced conversion in meetings held by German Reformed minister Philip Otterbein and Mennonite minister Martin Boehm. Their newfound pietism, in addition to their growing conviction that baptism should be by immersion, led them to form their own fellowship around 1778. While the group referred to itself as "Brethren," others, attempting to distinguish them from other Brethren groups in the area, called them the Brethren by the River (Susquehanna) or River Brethren. During the Civil War the leadership formally registered the group as Brethren in Christ. From their base in Pennsylvania, members spread to Canada (beginning in 1788), to the Midwest (by the 1840s) and, by the early 1900s, to California. These areas remain the centers of the Brethren in Christ Church.

By 1900 the Brethren in Christ had been deeply influenced by the American Holiness Movement, and in 1936 established Roxbury Holiness Camp, the first of four such camps now operated by the denomination. In 1887 a denominational paper, the *Evangelical Visitor*, was established, and in 1909 the first of four schools, Messiah Bible School and Missionary Training Home (now Messiah College, in Pennsylvania), was founded. In addition, the Brethren in Christ were active in Sunday school work and protracted revival meetings. Their missionary work, first begun in Africa and India, is now carried out on all continents except Australia.

Beginning in the late 1940s the Brethren in Christ moved closer to the conservative, evangelical mainstream of American religious life as they dropped requirements for plain dress and adopted a more ecumenical spirit by allowing open communion. By 1949 they were members of the National Association of Evangelicals and in 1950 joined the Christian Holiness Association. They retain such historic Anabaptist emphases as obedience, brotherhood and peace, and are active members of the Mennonite Central Committee. In 2002 there were 274 congregations in Canada and the U.S., with a combined membership of more than 23,000. The congregations are divided into six conferences, each headed by a bishop. A governing body, the General Conference, meets biannually.

431 Grantham Road, P. O. Box A
Grantham, PA 17027-0901
Phone: (717) 697-2634; Fax: (717) 697-7714
Website: www.bic-church.org

C

Canadian Baptist Ministries. A loose confederation of four autonomous Baptist Conventions/Unions. The founding denominations are the Convention of Atlantic Baptist Churches (538 churches), the Baptist Convention of Ontario and Quebec (382 churches), and the Baptist Union of Western Canada (162 churches). In 1970 the *Union d'Eglises baptistes françaises au Canada*, or Union of French Baptist Churches in Canada (29 churches), joined the confederation. Previously known as the Baptist Federation of Canada (1944) and the Canadian Baptist Federation (1983), in 1995 the Federation and Canadian Baptist International Ministries merged under the name Canadian Baptist Ministries (CBM). In 2003 the combined CBM membership was approximately 130,000.

Atlantic Baptists trace their history to the late 1800s when British Empire Loyalists emigrated following the American Revolution. Growth attributable to the Alline revivals and Free Will Baptist missionary enterprise eventually resulted in an Arminian stream that coalesced with Calvinistic Baptists to form the United Baptist Convention of the Maritime (now Atlantic) Provinces in 1905-1906. The Baptist Convention of Ontario and Quebec (1888) was organized in Upper and Lower Canada by Baptist emigrants from Britain and the U.S., the majority of them Particular Baptists. Baptist witness in Western Canada began in Manitoba in 1873 through the initiative of Ontario missionaries, and in British Columbia in 1875 with American Baptist support. In 1907 to 1909 four provincial conventions founded the Baptist Union of Western Canada. The *Union d'Eglises baptistes françaises au Canada* (1969) is the indigenous product of the historic Grand Ligne Mission. Canadian Baptists support four theological colleges, one junior college and two lay training institutes.

In the 1840s and in the decade of the 1900s, attempts were made to unite Baptists in Canada. However, it was only in 1944, in Saint John, New Brunswick, that the Federation emerged as a national coordinating agency. The structure is presbygational, with a twenty-six member council nominated by the convention/unions, but it is consensual in practice. An inspirational Triennial Assembly elects officers but lacks legislative or fiscal authority. In the 1920s the fundamentalist-modernist controversy produced schisms from the

Baptist Convention of Ontario and Quebec as well as the Baptist Union of Western Canada. In 1965 the resulting communions organized a second indigenous Baptist denomination, the Canada-wide Fellowship of Evangelical Baptist Churches.

Canadian Baptist Ministries cooperates with numerous relief agencies overseas. In Canada the CBM serves as the voice of Canadian Baptists before governments, and it provides ministerial support services and limited publication assistance.

7185 Millcreek Drive
Mississauga, Ontario L5N 5R4
Phone: (905) 821-3533; Fax: (905) 826-3441
Website: www.cbmin.org

Children of God. *See* Family, The.

Christian and Missionary Alliance. Evangelical denomination with strong emphases on overseas missions and personal holiness. The century-long history of The Christian and Missionary Alliance (C&MA) is essentially the story of a parachurch organization evolving into a denomination.

The founder of the movement, A. B. Simpson, was a Canadian-born Presbyterian minister. As pastor of a well-to-do church in New York City, Simpson began to gather like-minded people with a burning interest in evangelism, world missions and a deeper Christian life. After leaving his prestigious parish Simpson began a number of ministries: the Gospel Tabernacle, a nondenominational church (1881); the Missionary Training Institute (later, Nyack College, 1882); the Christian Alliance (1887); and the Evangelical Missionary Alliance (1887).

The Christian Alliance was envisioned by Simpson as a broad fellowship of Christians who, while retaining membership in their denominations and individual churches, would gather for fellowship and mutual encouragement. This ecumenically spirited fellowship focused on themes such as "the gospel of full salvation and present and complete sanctification" and "the provision Christ has made in the Gospel for our physical redemption through divine healing." The Evangelical Missionary Alliance was the missionary arm of this parent organization. Its role was to promote missions and send missionaries around the world. In 1897 the two alliances amalgamated into one organization, the Christian and Missionary Alliance.

The primary institutions of the movement were branches, local gatherings of people from varying churches and denominations, as well as national conventions of the various branches. Simpson had never intended to start new churches or a new denomination. But over the years this parachurch organization began to look more and more like a denomination. Many branches became actual churches, and people associated with the movement began churches which they designated as Christian and Missionary Alliance. By the 1960s its leadership had acknowledged that it was indeed a denomination.

Today the worldwide constituency of the Alliance is approximately two million members and adherents in over forty countries. In 2003 the denomination included nearly 2,000 churches with approximately 350,000 members and adherents. The U.S. headquarters for the Alliance is in Nyack, New York. The denomination owns and operates three colleges (Nyack College, Simpson College in San Francisco, and St. Paul Bible College in Minnesota) and Alliance Theological Seminary in New York, while the Canadian schools are Canadian Bible College and Canadian Theological Seminary in Regina, Saskatchewan.

The doctrinal statement of the C&MA includes such themes as the inerrancy of Scripture, sanctification as both a crisis and a progressive experience, physical healing and the imminent and premillennial return of Christ.

P.O. Box 35000
Colorado Springs, CO 80935-3500
Phone: (719) 599-5999; Fax: (719) 593-8692
Website: www.cmalliance.org

Christian Church (Disciples of Christ). A denomination arising out of the Restoration Movement. The Christian Church (Disciples of Christ) traces its roots to the Restoration Movement of the early nineteenth century, arising out of the 1831 merger between Barton W. Stone's "Christians" and Alexander Campbell's "Disciples" to form the Christian Church/Disciples of Christ. By the end of the nineteenth century the movement represented the fastest growing religious body in America and, until overtaken by the Mormons well into this century, the Christian Church (Disciples of Christ) was the largest indigenous American religious body.

Originally the movement was marked by two distinctive goals: to restore simple evangelical Christianity and to unite all truly Christian churches and denominations under the lordship of Jesus Christ and the authority of Scripture. But from the beginning of the movement, these dual emphases were held in tension. Although this fellowship of Christian Churches was one of the very few American religious bodies that did not split during the Civil War, the tension between primitivism and inclusivism had begun to fracture the movement by the late nineteenth century. By 1906 the U.S. Religious Census could distinguish between the more traditional Churches of Christ and the more liberal and inclusivist Disciples of Christ. This distinction was sealed in 1927 by the formation of the North American Christian Convention by the conservative Independents (*see* Christian Churches/Churches of Christ [Independent]).

Over most of its history the Christian Church (Disciples of Christ) has maintained the practices common to most Restoration churches: the local autonomy of individual congregations, the plurality of elders, Communion every Sunday and baptism by immersion for the remission of sins as a condition for church membership. Today, however, most congregations practice open membership and accept nonimmersed believers into fellowship as full members. Disciples continue to claim the Restoration tradition of having "no creed but Christ" and "no book but the Bible," but many do so within the context of modern biblical criticism. Congregations usually require for church membership only that prospective members make the "Good Confession" of Matthew 16:16.

In the twentieth century the Christian Church (Disciples of Christ) gradually recognized its denominational nature and took its place among mainline Protestant denominations. Today the Disciples have a regional and national structure. Always proponents of ecumenism, the Disciples were active in the founding of the Federal Council of Churches as well as the World Council of Churches and are members of Churches Uniting in Christ. During the past twenty-five years the Disciples, as have many mainline denominations, have experienced a numerical decline. In 2002 their national office reported 3,716 congregations in North America, with a total membership of 788,965.

130 East Washington Street
Indianapolis, IN 46204-3645
Phone: (317) 635-3100; Fax: (317) 635-3700
Website: www.disciples.org

Christian Church (Disciples of Christ) in Canada. A denomination in the Restoration tradition. The Disciples in Canada trace their origins to two separate streams of missionary enterprise: Scottish immigrants who were determined to follow strict New Testament polity and practice, and the Disciples of Christ, whose churches appeared in Ontario (c. 1820) and in Western Canada (1881).

The early Disciples were New Testament restorationists who espoused frontier ecumenism, eschewed creedal tests and practiced congregational polity. Arminian, postmillennial and revivalistic, most forwarded the "five finger" plan of salvation (faith, repentance, confession [of faith], baptism and the gift of the Holy Spirit) introduced by an associate of the Campbells, Walter Scott.

Disciples congregations are led by elders and deacons, and their clergy are ordained by one of the thirty-five regions. They observe the Lord's Supper weekly and believers' baptism by immersion. Historically their congregational polity militated against centralization, but communication through journals such as *The Christian Gleaner* (c. 1833), Halifax, and the *Gospel Vindicator* (1837), Cobourg, eventually led to the formation of "co-operations" or associations of churches. In 1922 an All-Canada Committee came into being. Disciples are charter members of the Canadian Council of Churches (1944), and they joined the World Council of Churches (1948). They were formal participants in the ill-fated General Commission on Church Union (1973) with the United and Anglican churches.

Two major schisms have taken place from the Disciples. In the nineteenth century, regional and theological tensions in the U.S. gave rise to the Churches of Christ (noninstrumentalists). Later protests over theological liberalism and social action led to organization of the North American Christian Convention (1927), popularly known as the Christian Churches. Both groups are relatively significant in Canada. In response to the restructuring of the denomination in 1968, about one-third of the churches ceased association. In 1987 the Disciples had nine churches in Atlantic Canada, seventeen in Ontario and eleven in Western Canada, with a membership of 4,700. In 2001 the Disciples had 26 churches with an inclusive membership of 2,493.

P.O. Box 23030, 417 Wellington St.
St. Thomas, Ontario N5R 6A3
Phone: (519) 633-9703; Fax: (519) 637-6407
Website: www.web.net/~disciple

Christian Churches/Churches of Christ (Independent). An association of churches arising out of the Restoration Movement. The Christian Churches/Churches of Christ (Independent) trace their roots to the Restoration Movement of the early nineteenth century, arising out of the 1831 merger between Barton W. Stone's "Christians" and Alexander Campbell's "Disciples" to form the Christian Church/Disciples of Christ.

Tensions between strict and progressive restorationists became apparent by the end of the nineteenth century. By 1906 the U.S. Religious Census had recognized a distinction between more strict Churches of Christ and the Disciples of Christ. In 1927 a group that objected to the liberalism of the International Convention of the Disciples met in Memphis to form the North American Christian Convention. Not intending to withdraw from fellowship with other restorationist churches, these conservatives, or "Independents" as they were called, developed a direct-support missionary program, Christian service camps and several educational institutions, the most prominent being Cincinnati Bible Seminary and Lincoln Christian College and Seminary. In the late 1960s conservative leaders made a concerted effort to have all independent congregations withdraw their names from the Disciples of Christ *Year Book*, a published list of local congregations within the movement.

The Christian Churches/Churches of Christ have always had much in common with the mainstream of evangelicalism, particularly in their understanding of Scripture as a divinely inspired and sufficient revelation and in their opposition to theological liberalism. However, they have also remained insulated from the controversies over issues such as millennialism, perfectionism and glossolalia that have marked the larger evangelical tradition in America. Doctrinally, the Independents have also been distinguished by their belief in the necessity of baptism by immersion for the remission of sins as a condition for church membership (in obedience to what they believe to be the injunction of Acts 2:38). But in recent years there has been a growing tension within the churches over the theology of baptism. While some suggest a theology approximating baptismal regeneration, others, still maintaining a high view of baptism, stop well short of making water baptism regenerative. According to the *Directory of the Ministry of the Christian Churches and Churches of Christ,* in 2000 they had more than 5,000 congregations and a total membership of 1,072,000.

P.O. Box 749
San Mateo, CA 94401
Phone: (650) 558-9596
Website: www.church-of-christ.org

Christian Holiness Association. An association of Holiness churches, originally known as the National Campmeeting Association for the Promotion of Christian Holiness. In 1867 several Methodist ministers at a camp meeting in Vineland, New Jersey, called for the promotion of the doctrine of holiness (also known as "entire sanctification," Christian perfection or the "second blessing"). Impressed by the success of the meeting, these ministers organized the National Campmeeting Association for the Promotion of Christian Holiness in its aftermath.

In its early years the Association was a close-knit circle of Methodist revivalists who served as pastors during the winter months. They owned no property or facilities, but convened revival meetings when invited by local, state or district camp meeting committees. These committees often were part of state or local Holiness associations, the organization of which had been encouraged by the National Association. Between 1867 and 1883 some fifty-two meetings were held in such places as Asbury Grove, Massachusetts; Mannheim, Pennsylvania; and Des Plaines, Illinois.

The Association began as an evangelistic organization with the special task of restoring what it regarded as John Wesley's teaching on Christian perfection. Camp meeting revivalism was the Association's principal method. However, it also published books and periodicals in support of the Holiness cause.

In 1971 the group changed its name to the Christian Holiness Association. By this time it had evolved into an association of Holiness churches and later sponsored its own scholarly fellowship, the Wesleyan Theological Society. More conservative members of the Association expressed their growing dissatisfaction with relaxed discipline by forming, after 1955, the Interdenominational Holiness Convention.

Christian Methodist Episcopal Church. An African American Methodist denomination. Formally organized in 1870 by the remaining African American members of the Methodist Episcopal Church, South (MECS), the Colored Methodist Episcopal Church (CME)—its official name until 1954—was the fourth African American denomination to separate from biracial but proscriptive connections in nineteenth-century American Methodism. The product of both the Southern Methodist program to evangelize the slaves and the African American initiative to embrace the Christian faith despite the social system of slavery, the CME Church evolved at local and annual conference levels, beginning in 1867. The members of the CME had refused to join the African Methodist Episcopal (AME) and African Methodist Episcopal Zion (AMEZ) denominations, or the Northern-based Methodist Episcopal Church as it returned to the South after the Civil War. Cooperating with their former masters, they adopted the theology and polity of the MECS and received title to church property from white trustees. Disavowing political activism during Reconstruction, the new church had, and has kept, a Southern base in Tennessee. Its first seven bishops were born in slavery.

Accompanying Southern African Americans as they migrated north, the CME Church expanded to eighteen Northern and Western states. The denomination authorized an order of deaconesses in 1894, channeled the energies of female members into the Women's Missionary Council in 1918 and opened ordination to women later in the century. It supported a number of church schools in the South, including Paine, Lane, Texas, Miles and Mississippi Industrial colleges, and the Phillips Theological Seminary, now part of the Interdenominational Theological Center in Atlanta. Its denominational paper, *The Christian Index,* is the second-oldest continuing African American religious periodical in the country.

In the twentieth century the CME Church has moved into the mainstream of African American social and political involvement, with public condemnations of lynching, cooperation with the civil rights programs, and participation in the Social Gospel orientation of the Federal (later National) Council of Churches. The denomination has also been active in world Methodist organizations and ecumenical discussions, the Churches Uniting in Christ and merger proposals with the AME and AMEZ churches.

Numbering more than 800,000 members, the CME Church is organized into thirty-eight annual conferences in thirty-four states, besides conferences in Ghana and Nigeria and missions in Haiti.

4466 Elvis Presley Blvd., Suite 137
Memphis, TN 38116
Website: www.c-m-e.org

Christian Reformed Church in North America. A small Reformed denomination, principally of Dutch descent, centered in the American Midwest. The Christian Reformed Church (CRC) grew out of the later (1840s-1920s) wave of Dutch immigration to the United States. Although the first arrivals affiliated with the *Reformed Church in America, some seceded in 1857 to form the "True Dutch Reformed Church." The group became a viable enterprise only around 1880 with the resurgence of Dutch immigration and a second defection from the Reformed Church in America, this time over the issue of Freemasonry.

For the next fifty years, the church, now called the Christian Reformed Church, continued this strategy of absorbing the disaffected (in New Jersey) and the recently immigrated (extending to the West Coast). It moved into Canada with the post-World War II Dutch migration there, so that Canadians constitute over a quarter of its current membership (279,000, including baptized children, in 989 congregations). More recent additions have come from outside the Dutch circle, consisting of many African Americans but largely Korean-Americans.

While the language change from Dutch to English was completed in the 1930s, the CRC has been consistently defined by traits from its Netherlandic past. It stresses (1) heartfelt conversion and piety, although cast in covenantal rather than revivalistic terms, (2) confessionalism and orthodoxy, as set by its three standards—the Belgic Confession, the Heidelberg Catechism and the Canons of Dort, and (3) Christian cultural engagement. The latter emphasis was enunciated by the Dutch Neo-Calvinist forebear Abraham Kuyper and is exemplified in the denomination's longstanding Christian day school system, as well as its academic and political leadership in recent American evangelicalism. Its postsecondary educational institutions are Calvin College and Calvin Seminary in Grand Rapids, Michigan.

2850 Kalamazoo Ave. SE
Grand Rapids, MI 49560
Phone: (616) 241-1691
Website: www.crcna.org

Christian Science. *See* Church of Christ, Scientist.

Church of Christ, Scientist. An indigenous American religion noted for its theory and practice of religious healing. Christian Science was born in 1866 when Mary Baker Eddy's spontaneous recovery from a severe injury authenticated her discovery that reality is completely spiritual, and evil (including sickness and death) is an illusion. There is no reality except Mind and Spirit. The result is that the essential orthodox Christian doctrines of creation, fall and redemption are denied. All Christian Scientists practice healing by "demonstrating" over (curing) "false claims" (sickness and sin), but some devote themselves professionally to full-time service as practitioners. Christian Science church services do not permit preaching, but are carried out by first and second readers who read selections from Scripture and from *Science and Health*.

Despite Eddy's teaching and the publication of her textbook *Science and Health* (1875), to which *Key to the Scriptures* was added in 1883, Christian Science grew slowly. In 1879 she moved her headquarters from Lynn, Massachusetts, to Boston. In 1892 Eddy established a central church organization, the Mother Church, in Boston and appointed a board of directors to oversee its affairs and implement her instructions to organize evangelistic lectures and monitor educational standards. Six years later Eddy founded the Christian Science Publishing Society to spearhead worldwide evangelism through the printed word, including *The Christian Science Monitor* (1908). These missionary activities enhanced the growth of Christian Science, spreading it to Europe and Asia by the early twentieth century. Membership exploded from only 8,724 in 1890 to about 55,000 (72 percent of whom were women) by 1906, and the U.S. Government Census of 1936 reported 268,915 Christian Science adherents. Although no more recent statistics are available because Eddy forbade their publication, local churches now number about 2,000 worldwide, with the vast majority of Christian Scientists still in the U.S.

175 Huntington Ave.
Boston, MA 02115
Phone: (615) 450-2000
Website: www.tfccs.com

Church of God (Anderson, Indiana). The Church of God (Anderson) is the largest of the Holiness groups bearing the name. Daniel Sydney Warner experienced sanctification in 1877 and was disfellowshiped a year later from the General Eldership of the Church of God in North America because of his emphasis on entire sanctification. He then joined an offshoot of this group, the Northern Indiana Eldership of the Church of God, which was open to Holiness teaching. When this group refused to adopt Warner's proposal to ban both pastoral licenses and church membership, he announced his freedom from all sects and was joined by five other individuals. This action, in October 1881, is generally considered the beginning of the Church of God. Persons from various denominations heeded Warner's call to reject sectarianism and "come out" from them.

Warner opposed all forms of ecclesiastical organization, including formal church membership, arguing that only God knows who the true Christians are. Ordination was simply a recognition of the reception of a divine call to preach and would be granted by a committee of state or regional pastors. This emphasis on the guidance of the Holy Spirit accounts for the fact that women have always been ordained by the movement.

Development of the Church of God was hindered by its opposition to organization. Gradually, the group has accepted the argument that while the church itself cannot be organized, it is expedient to organize the work of the church. Currently, nine agencies serve this function. A General Ministerial Assembly, begun in 1917 and renamed the General Assembly, consists of ministers and some laypeople. It cannot speak for the whole movement, so its resolutions are not binding. Each congregation is independent and calls its own pastor.

The Bible serves as the group's creed and is regarded as infallible in matters of faith and life. The doctrines of holiness and unity were the major theological themes of the new movement. Initially, the group was known as "church of God," with a lowercase *c* to indicate its inclusion of all Christians. The early leaders insisted they were restoring primitive Christianity rather than founding a denomination. The group continues to reject a denominational designation, preferring to be called a movement. Arminian in orientation, the church teaches faith healing and a doctrine of the second coming of Christ unaccompanied by a millennium. Three ordinances are practiced: baptism by immersion, Communion, which is open to all believers, and foot washing.

The *Gospel Trumpet* (renamed *Vital Christianity* in 1962) has provided a vital function in the growth of the church, supplemented by itinerant preachers, called "flying messengers," during the early years of the movement. Since 1906 the *Gospel Trumpet* has been published in Anderson, Indiana, which in turn became the national headquarters for the Church of God. While congregations primarily emerged in rural areas, at least forty-five missionary homes operated in urban areas between 1890 and the early 1920s. These homes served as training centers and provided experience in urban ministries. Realizing the need for formal education for pastors, Anderson Bible Training School (now Anderson University) opened in 1917. The School of Theology was added in 1950. The church supports several colleges in the U.S.

The Missionary Committee, established in 1909, by 1987 could count 229,258 adherents in sixty-two countries outside the U.S. Since 1947 the movement has sponsored the Christian Brotherhood Hour, a radio program broadcast in the U.S. and abroad. In 2003 there were 2,300 congregations in the U.S. and Canada with an average of 235,000 in worship.

P.O. Box 2420
Anderson, IN 46018-2420
Phone: (800) 848-2464; Fax: (765) 642-5652
Website: www.chog.org

Church of God (Cleveland, Tennessee). The Church of God (Cleveland, Tennessee) is the oldest Pentecostal church in the U.S. In 1886 eight people formed the Christian Union in Tennessee with the goal of restoring primitive Christianity, promoting Holiness doctrine and uniting all denominations. The Christian Union chose Richard G. Spurling Jr. as its pastor. The church joined with another group in North Carolina in 1896. Church members first spoke in tongues at services near Camp Creek, North Carolina, in 1896 under the ministry of W. F. Bryant, a layperson.

Originally opposed to organization, the group adopted a simple plan of government in 1902 to guard against fanaticism. At that time, it adopted the name The Holiness Church at Camp Creek, abandoning its mission to bring all denominations together. The group endured, despite early persecution from mobs who threw rocks at members' houses, burned churches and whipped members.

Ministers met yearly in various churches as a general assembly from 1906 until 1916 when an auditorium in Harriman, Tennessee, was purchased for this purpose. In 1920 a new auditorium was built in Cleveland, Tennessee, and while the general assembly has met in various locations since 1934, the general headquarters remain in Cleveland. As the church grew, so did the organization, and the office of general moderator was established in 1909, renamed general overseer a year later. The duties of this position included the appointment of pastors. State overseers were first appointed in 1911. A Council of Twelve, established in 1917, assists the general overseer and plans the agenda for the general assembly of pastors. All ordained ministers meet prior to the general assembly and discuss issues presented by the Council of Twelve. Their recommendations are generally accepted by the entire general assembly.

Originally decrying creeds, in 1948 the church formulated a Declaration of Faith affirming belief in the verbal inspiration of the Bible, the premillennial second coming of Christ and divine healing. Three ordinances, baptism by immersion, the Lord's Supper and foot washing, are practiced. The church has maintained its Holiness doctrine of sanctification but believes that this experience is followed by the baptism of the Spirit, evidenced by speaking in tongues. The church is a member of the National Association of Evangelicals.

Ordained ministers were called bishops until 1948. Women serve as evangelists and preachers but are not ordained. In 1910 the Church of God established its Bible Training School, which was relocated in Cleveland, Tennessee, in 1947, and is now known as Lee College. Over the years the Church of God has experienced numerous splits resulting in several independent groups, also bearing the name Church of God. In 1987 there were 505,755 members in the U.S. worshiping in 5,346 churches. In 2003 the churches had expanded to 6,196, and worldwide the church had over 6 million members in 150 countries.

P.O. Box 2430
Cleveland, TN 37320-2430
Phone: (423) 472-3361; Fax: (423) 478-7066
Website: www.chofgod.org

Church of God in Christ. The Church of God in Christ (COGIC), with headquarters in Memphis, Tennessee, is the largest African American Pentecostal group in the world. Its founder was Charles H. Mason, who was licensed by the Missionary Baptist Church in 1893. Claiming to experience entire sanctification that same year, he was expelled by the Baptists. In 1895 Mason and Charles P. Jones founded the Church of Christ (Holiness) U.S.A., a group emphasizing entire sanctification. Mason also began a congregation in Lexington, Mississippi, in 1897, which he called the Church of God in Christ as a result of his conviction that this was the appropriate biblical name.

In 1907 Mason traveled to Los Angeles to witness the Azusa Street revival, and there he first spoke in tongues. During the general assembly of the Church of Christ (Holiness) U.S.A., Mason introduced the new Pentecostal doctrine. The non-Pentecostal faction, led by Jones, withdrew and retained the name Church of Christ (Holiness) U.S.A. The majority remained with Mason who, along with D. J. Young, called together African American preachers who believed in speaking in tongues. Meeting in Memphis, Tennessee, in August 1907, they organized themselves as a general assembly of the Church of God in Christ. Mason was elected to serve as the general overseer, and Young became editor of the group's newspaper, *Whole Truth.*

From its inception COGIC has been governed by a council of apostles and elders, in keeping with its understanding of the governance of the New Testament church. Emphasis is placed on the role of the Holy Spirit in directing the leadership. As general overseer and chief apostle, Mason maintained full control over the church. He appointed overseers for the various jurisdictions, as well as heads of the national departments. After his death in 1961, the issue of authority preoccupied the church. In 1968 a constitutional convention decided that a general board of twelve bishops, elected for a four-year term by the general assembly, would oversee the work of the church. The general assembly would also elect a presiding bishop and two assistants. The Church of God in Christ engaged in its first general election that same year. As a result of this change in policy, fourteen bishops of the church withdrew and organized the Church of God in Christ (International) in 1969 with headquarters in Kansas City, Missouri.

The Church of God in Christ is trinitarian and premillennialist. The church believes in divine healing and that tongues is a gift for all Christians, not just an elite few. Baptism is by immersion, and the church practices Communion and foot washing. Church members engage in an active worship style that includes dancing and shaking, practices they defend on biblical grounds. COGIC sponsors Saints Junior College in Lexington, Mississippi. In 1997 the church reported an estimated 8 million members.

938 Mason Street
Memphis, TN 38126
Phone: (901) 522-1331
Website: www.cogic.org

Church of God in Christ, Mennonite. A small, conservative Mennonite denomination. The group was founded by John Holdeman, who left the main body of Mennonites when they failed to ordain him. Holdeman began preaching on his own in 1859 and formed his own following.

Self-educated, fluent in English and in German, and able in Dutch and Greek, Holdeman became a firm adherent of the traditional Mennonite practice of maintaining a strictly disciplined church, including the shunning of excommunicated members. He also emphasized the new birth, the ministry of the Holy Spirit and strict separation from the world. Holdeman's followers were drawn from the *Mennonite Church as well as the Dutch Mennonite immigrants who had lived a few generations in Russia before coming to America. To this day the group is often referred to as the Holdeman Mennonites.

Like the Mennonite Church, they baptize only those who can claim repentance from sin and faith in Christ. All oaths are refused and the ethic of nonresistance is strictly adhered to. The church, the body of Christ, is to be holy, as its Lord is. As a symbol of nonconformity the men wear a neatly trimmed beard and no ties; the women wear full dresses, plain in character and without ornamentation. All jewelry is shunned. Higher education is not permitted. The Holdeman Mennonites are found mostly in North America and number about 12,000 baptized members in some 111 congregations.

P.O. Box 313, 420 N. Wedel Ave.
Moundridge, KS 67107
Phone: (620) 345-2532; Fax: (620) 345-2582
Website: http://holdeman.cjb.net (unofficial)

Church of God of Prophecy. Ambrose J. Tomlinson joined the *Church of God (Cleveland, Tennessee) in 1903 and was the body's first General Moderator. As the years passed, Tomlinson assumed increasing leadership until 1923, when the church impeached him on fifteen charges, including disloyalty, usurpation of authority and misappropriation of funds. Relieved of his duties, Tomlinson founded a rival church in Cleveland, Tennessee, known as Tomlinson Church of God. At his death in 1943 the church chose for its leader Milton R. Tomlinson, one of Tomlinson's two sons.

Milton R. Tomlinson led the group, now known as the Church of God of Prophecy, which maintained its headquarters in Cleveland, Tennessee. In the early 2000s membership in the Church of God of Prophecy was 75,000. From 1990 to 2000, the worldwide membership grew from 262,000 to 546,000. The Church of God of All Nations is a splinter movement that separated from the Church of God of

Prophecy in 1957 under the leadership of G. R. Kent.
   P. O. Box 2910
   Cleveland, TN 37320-2910
   Phone: (423) 559-5246
   Website: www.cogop.org

Church of God (Seventh Day). Adventists who refused to endorse Ellen White's visions and writings departed from her church in 1858 and organized the General Conference of the Church of God in 1884. "Seventh Day" was added to the name in 1923, reflecting their observance of the sabbath on the seventh day of the week. The church's offices were in Stanberry, Missouri, until 1950, when they relocated to Denver. A rival faction, keeping the same name, established headquarters in Salem, West Virginia, in 1933. Most members of the church in Salem reunited with the Denver group in 1949, but a small number with the same name are still headquartered in Salem. The Denver group reports 165 congregations in 2003.
   P. O. Box 3367
   Denver, CO 80233
   Phone: (303) 452-7973
   Website: www.cog7.org

Church of Jesus Christ of Latter-day Saints (Mormons). A new religion founded in the nineteenth century by Joseph Smith. The Church of Christ, which became the Church of Jesus Christ of Latter-day Saints (LDS), or Mormonism, was established on April 6, 1830, at Fayette, in the "burned-over district" of upstate New York, by Joseph Smith, following the publication of the Book of Mormon on March 26, 1830. Smith claimed to have derived the book from golden plates that he had discovered with the aid of the angel Moroni. The plates, Smith said, were written in "Reformed Egyptian," which he translated with the aid of two stones through which he viewed the writings. As a new prophet of God, Smith gathered a following of devoted disciples. In 1840 the Mormon apostle Orson Pratt published an account of an encounter between Smith, God the Father and Jesus Christ, said to have taken place as early as 1820. Today the story of this "first vision" has become one of the basic apologetic claims of Mormonism.

The Book of Mormon, among other things, revealed America as a new land of promise and traced the fortunes of pre-Columbian immigrants to America: the Jaredites, the Lamanites (Native Americans) and the Nephites. After numerous battles between these groups, the righteous Nephites had been reduced by the Lamanites to only Mormon and his son, Moroni, who buried their book in A.D. 384 to await the day when God would raise up their spiritual descendants.

From the beginning Smith strove to develop economically strong communities, a practice his successors continued with great success, making the economic base of Mormonism the source of its evangelism. One of the early converts was Sidney Rigdon, a Campbellite Restorationist who had gathered a small community in Kirtland, Ohio. Rigdon and nearly all of his followers were baptized into the Mormon faith, and by 1831 Kirtland had become the first holy city of Smith's new church. But by 1838 the Kirtland community suffered economic collapse, and Smith fled with others to Jackson County, Missouri, where the Lord had revealed to Smith that he should build "an holy city, which should be called Zion." However, the group faced repeated and violent conflict with local residents and civil authorities. Fleeing to Illinois, they established a settlement at Nauvoo.

Smith's downfall came with his teachings about polygamy, which he advanced as a secret ordinance. Smith appears to have begun this practice as early as 1836 and to have married at least forty-nine women, including the wives of several of his disciples. His adulterous advances led four disillusioned converts to found the anti-Mormon newspaper *The Nauvoo Expositor*, which exposed his secret life and teachings. His brothers instigated a riot that destroyed the newspaper office. As a result, Smith and one brother, Hyrum, were arrested. They were murdered on June 27, 1844, by a lynch mob.

Following Smith's death, his disciples split into over twenty-five different groups, all of which claimed to follow his true teachings. The main division was between those who followed his brother William and eventually his son Joseph Smith III, and those who followed Brigham Young. In 1847 Young led the Mormons on their famous migration to the Salt Lake area of what would become the state of Utah (1896).

Branches of Mormonism. Today the largest group is the Utah Mormons based in Salt Lake City. In 2003 there were approximately 5,410,000 Utah Mormons in North America and over 11,700,000 worldwide. They are distinguished by their acceptance of the leadership of Brigham Young and his successors.

The other main branch of Mormonism is the smaller Community of Christ, whose headquarters is in Independence, Missouri. (Until April 6, 2001, the Community of Christ was known as the Reorganized Church of Jesus Christ of Latter-day Saints.) This group was supported by Joseph Smith's legal wife, Emma, and legitimated its claims on the basis of lineal descent from Joseph Smith. In 2003 it had about 250,000 members. From the beginning it completely rejected polygamy and even tried to claim that Joseph Smith had not practiced it. Theologically it is closer to orthodox Christianity than the Utah Mormons.

In addition, there are still several fundamentalist sectarian groups, such as the Bickertonites, Strangites and Temple Lot Churches, which generally hold to the teachings of the Book of Mormon and early Mormon doctrines but reject later developments as unscriptural innovations. There are also numerous groups of Utah fundamentalists who continue the practice of polygamy and claim that the Utah Church hierarchy has deviated from its calling for pragmatic reasons. These groups usually exist under the leadership of a prophet. Mormon fundamentalist groups have around 25,000 followers.

Mormon beliefs and practices. Utah Mormonism is an indigenous religious movement that incorporates American values of self-reliance, pragmatism, progress and democracy. It fits into the religious context of early nineteenth-century New England, which produced the Oneida Community and a host of other communal experiments based on a theology of human perfectibility and an implicit belief in the essential divinity of humankind.

The Book of Mormon is fundamentally an early-American romance based on the Bible. LDS missionaries stress the importance of the Bible and the Book of Mormon as sources for their beliefs, downplaying the role of continuing revelation characteristic of their church. Yet in reality they read both the Bible and the Book of Mormon in light of later revelations given to Joseph Smith and successive prophets. These include *Doctrine and Covenants* and *The Pearl of Great Price* as well as other revelations given to church leaders since Smith's death.

Structurally, Latter-day Saints theology is held together by an evolutionary framework known as the doctrine of eternal progression. This belief is summed up by the phrase "As man is, God once was; as God is, man may become." Thus human destiny is to evolve to Godhood through obedience to the laws and ordinances revealed to the LDS church. Spiritual progress is, however, conditional on choices made by the individual, making LDS theology an extreme form of Arminianism at best. The doctrine of eternal progression and claims by Brigham Young and other early leaders that Adam was the God of this earth also opens the door to criticism of insipient polytheism. Some Mormon scholars, however, point out that these are not part of official LDS doctrine.

Belief in preexistent souls and the existence of various heavenly realms endow Utah Mormonism with a system of rewards that motivate individuals to participate in elaborate temple ceremonies. In many respects these practices reflect the influences of popular religious (both orthodox and unorthodox) and scientific beliefs of the early nineteenth century. However, contrary to sensational claims by some evangelical writers, there seems to be no evidence that Mormon temple rites involve explicit Satanism.

Recently, the Latter-day Saints have made a concerted effort to become part of mainstream America, and it appears that they are succeeding. In spite of their unconventional past and the doctrinal, social and scientific problems that continue to dog them, they are known as a socially and politically conservative, morally respectable, clean-living, industrious and family-oriented people.

Mormons and their church have had difficulty living down a couple of questionable social teachings from their past (although these seem to have had little effect on the church's growth). First is the issue of polygamy. It is historically established that Joseph Smith practiced and taught polygamy. It is also clear that this doctrine was central to his entire theological system and is an "everlasting covenant" (*Doctrine and Covenants*, sec. 132). In 1890 under the leadership of their president, Wilford Woodruff (1807-1898), the Utah Mormons officially declared, "We are not teaching polygamy or plural marriage, nor permitting any person to enter into its practice." This was done in order to reach a political accommodation with the U.S. government. And in 1904 the LDS leadership forbade their members to enter into new polygamous relationships. A few small splinter groups, however, continue to be polygamous, and occasional media reports to this effect plague the Latter-day Saints.

Second, reflecting the predominant attitudes of the nineteenth century, Joseph Smith clearly taught that African Americans could not enter the Mormon priesthood—an office held by most male church members. This racial segregationism, however, was countered in 1978, when President Spencer W. Kimball reported that he had received a revelation from God extending the priesthood to *all* male members. Yet another example of continuing revelation correcting past infelicities can be seen in changes made to 2 Nephi 30:6 of the Book of Mormon, where God is said to promise to make certain Native Americans "a white and delightsome people." Since 1978 the wording has read *pure* instead of *white.*

From the beginning Christians have rejected Mormon claims to be a Christian church. Major differences remain in the doctrines of God, salvation, Scripture and eternal destinies, to name but a few. Although most Mormons sincerely believe that they are Christians, the differences between the teachings of the Latter-day Saints and traditional Christianity are so great that most, if not all, other North American denominations do not officially recognize the LDS as a Christian church.

Church of Jesus Christ of Latter-day Saints
50 East North Temple
Salt Lake City, UT 84150
Phone: (801) 240-1000
Website: www.lds.org

Church of the Brethren. Founded in 1708 by Alexander Mack and seven others in Schwarzenau/Eder, Germany, as an Anabaptist/pietist sect, by 1719 persecution had forced a group to immigrate to Pennsylvania under the leadership of Peter Becker. It was not until 1729 that Mack arrived in Germantown, along with a group he had led to Holland in 1720, and assumed leadership of the Brethren in America. By the late eighteenth century the Brethren had followed the westward movement and settled in eastern Missouri, and by the mid-nineteenth century they could be found on the Great Plains and West Coast. By 1948 the Brethren had become an ecumenically oriented Free Church known for its service outreach and peace emphasis. In 1999 the Church of the Brethren had about 138,000 adult members in over 1,000 congregations in the U.S., with a rapidly growing daughter church in Nigeria created by missions efforts. Congregations in other former mission areas have joined united churches in India, China and Ecuador.

A historic peace church since 1935, the Brethren organized in 1941 a service committee that developed worldwide activity in relief and rehabilitation programs. Among the Brethren-initiated projects that found interdenominational support were the Christian Rural Overseas Program (CROP), Heifer Project International and International Christian Youth Exchange (ICYE).

Brethren resist creedal statements but accept basic Protestant doctrines. In patterning church life after the early Christians, they practice several ordinances. These include (1) believer's baptism by threefold immersion (earning them the nickname "Dunkers"), (2) the love feast (following John 13), incorporating a time of examination, foot washing, a fellowship meal and partaking of bread and cup, (3) affirmation instead of oath taking, and (4) the laying on of hands. Brethren teach a simple, nonconforming way of life; until 1911 the church required a prescribed plain dress.

Brethren polity combines congregational and presbyterian elements, with an authoritative annual conference. Staff workers located at Elgin, Illinois, and New Windsor, Maryland, carry out church programs under the direction of an elected General Board. The denomination was a charter member of the National Council of Churches of Christ in 1950 (having joined the Federal Council in 1941) and of the World Council of Churches in 1948.

1451 Dundee Ave.
Elgin, IL 60120
Phone: (800) 323-8039
Website: www.brethren.org

Church of the Nazarene. A denomination originating from the union of several religious bodies with roots in the nineteenth-century Holiness Movement. Consonant with its origins, the Church of the Nazarene emphasizes the doctrine of entire sanctification as a second definite work of grace subsequent to conversion and advocates a disciplined lifestyle for its members reflecting "holiness of heart and life."

The Church of the Nazarene began in the U.S. as a result of the proliferation of independent Holiness associations, missions and churches during the second half of the nineteenth century and early part of the twentieth century. Eventually, a "union movement" favoring a national Holiness church arose among some of these bodies, encouraged notably by Phineas F. Bresee, a former Methodist pastor and presiding elder who organized the first group to use the name Church of the Nazarene in Los Angeles in 1895. Bresee's group, and a group of Holiness churches in the East, the Association of Pentecostal Churches in America, united in Chicago in 1907 to form the Pentecostal Church of the Nazarene. This body subsequently united in 1908 with the Holiness Church of Christ, a Southern group, at Pilot Point, Texas. The name remained Pentecostal Church of the Nazarene for a time, but in 1919 the term *Pentecostal* was dropped due to its association with tongues speaking, a practice not endorsed by the Church of the Nazarene.

Doctrinally the Church of the Nazarene has been shaped most by that branch of the Christian tradition associated with John Wesley and his Methodist movement. Wesley's teaching, especially his doctrine of Christian perfection, was central to the Holiness Movement. Among the fifteen articles of faith in the church's *Manual* are belief in the Holy Scriptures, which "inerrantly reveal the will of God concerning us in all things necessary to our salvation"; belief that through grace all persons who will may "turn from sin to righteousness" and "believe on Jesus Christ for pardon and cleansing from sin"; and belief in entire sanctification as "that act of God, subsequent to regeneration, by which believers are made free from original sin, or depravity, and brought into a state of entire devotement to God, and the holy obedience of love made perfect," an act "wrought by the baptism with the Holy Spirit." Divine healing is affirmed although not to the exclusion of medical means. Both infant and adult believer's baptism are provided for, and belief in the second coming of Christ is held to be essential to Christian faith.

The *Manual* also contains "General" and "Special Rules" according to which members pledge themselves to "feeding the hungry, clothing the naked, visiting the sick and imprisoned, and ministering to the needy" as well as "avoiding evil of every kind," including profaning the Lord's Day; using alcohol, tobacco or drugs; the "indulging of pride in dress or behavior"; and "entertainments which are subversive of the Christian ethic."

Local churches retain considerable congregational autonomy while at the same time they are subject to oversight by both district superintendents and general superintendents. Ultimate authority in the church is held by the general assembly, an elected body of both laypersons and clergy, which meets usually every four years. In addition, a general board of both clergy and lay people elected by the general assembly oversees the work of the church in the time between general-assembly meetings.

Strongly committed to world missions from its beginning, the church now has work in 135 world areas, with an international membership of 1,466,920 throughout 12,673 congregations (as of 2002). Of this total, 643,649 are in the U.S., 12,673 in Canada, and 121,936 in Mexico and Central America. With international headquarters in Kansas City, Missouri, the church operates a publishing house, a graduate theological seminary, nine liberal-arts colleges in the U.S. and Canada and two colleges in Europe, as well as numerous schools, hospitals and clinics in various other parts of the world.

6401 The Paseo
Kansas City, MO 64131
Phone: (816) 333-7000; Fax: (816) 822-9071
Website: www.nazarene.org

Church of the New Jerusalem. A religious body founded on the spiritual teachings of Emanuel Swedenborg. Swedish scientist Emanuel Swedenborg (1688-1772) claimed to have had a revelation that enabled him to communicate with the world of spirits and angels, through whom he claimed to have learned the secrets of the universe. Swedenborg accepted a canon of twenty-nine books of the Old Testament and five books of the New and attempted to move beyond their literal and historical meaning to extract their spiritual or allegorical meaning. He seems to have denied the orthodox doctrine of the Trinity (teaching that God is one in three principles, each of which are manifest in Jesus Christ), original sin, the vicarious atonement and the bodily resurrection; but some individual congregations of the church do not appear to be quite so unorthodox.

Based on the teachings of Swedenborg, Robert Hindmarsh launched the New Jerusalem Church in London in the 1780s, and churches were established in England, Sweden, Germany and North America. The churches exist in three main bodies today: the General Conference in England, The General Convention of the New Jerusalem in the U.S.A. and the General Church of the New Jerusalem, which in 1890 broke from the parent group in the U.S.

The General Convention had 2,029 members in thirty-one societies in 2000 and maintains a theological school at Newton, Massachusetts. The General Church had 5,563 members in 2000, meeting in twenty-one organized circles and fifteen organized groups. It maintains a theological school, a college and a secondary school, and its headquarters are at Bryn Athyn, Pennsylvania. The General Convention has self-regulating societies holding services based on the *Book of Worship* of the Convention. There is an annual meeting. It subscribes to the belief "that there is one God, in whom there is a Divine Trinity; and that He is the Lord Jesus Christ" and "that saving faith is to believe on Him." The General Church accepts the full authority of the writings of Swedenborg and has no fixed constitution. Church organization is based on "essential unanimity" in free council and assembly. Both U.S. branches have pastors. There is a Swedenborg Foundation in New York City which distributes the writings of Swedenborg, published in thirty volumes. Swedenborg's followers have included William Blake and Helen Keller, and his teachings influenced the work of Coleridge, Balzac and others.

P.O. Box 743
Bryn Athyn, PA 19009
Phone: (877) 411-HOPE (US)
Website: www.newchurch.org

Church of the United Brethren in Christ. An evangelical denomination with roots in German-American revivalism. The church be-

gan in 1800 as a result of the preaching of Martin Boehm and William Otterbein among Germans in Pennsylvania, Maryland and
Virginia. Methodist in doctrine, church government and practice, it
followed a Discipline patterned on the Methodist *Discipline.* The denomination split in 1889, primarily over proposed constitutional
changes permitting members to join lodges and secret societies. The
majority, or "new constitution," group joined with the Evangelical
Church in 1946 to become the Evangelical United Brethren Church.
That body then merged with the Methodist Church in 1968 to form
the *United Methodist Church.

The continuing Church of the United Brethren in Christ (Old
Constitution) retains its Methodist heritage, with a belief in the Trinity; the deity, humanity and atonement of Christ; and a lifestyle that
forbids alcoholic beverages, membership in secret societies and en-
gaging in aggressive (but not defensive) war. Its form of government follows that of the Methodist Church, and both men and
women can be ordained to the ministry. The denomination maintains a college and Graduate School of Christian Ministries in Huntington, Indiana, and supports missionary ventures in Sierra Leone,
Jamaica, Honduras and Hong Kong. Evangelical in orientation, the
church holds membership in the National Association of Evangelicals. In 1997 the denomination claimed 25,000 members in 250
churches.

302 Lake St.
Huntington, IN 46750
Phone: (260) 356-231
Website: www.ub.org

Churches of Christ (Non-Instrumental). A brotherhood of churches
spawned by the nineteenth-century Restoration Movement. The
Churches of Christ, first recognized as a distinct group in the 1906
federal census, tend to be the most conservative of the three groups
(including the Disciples of Christ and the *Christian Churches) arising out of the Restoration Movement.

The Churches of Christ retain Restorationist motifs from early
stages of the movement, which according to Alexander Campbell's
Millennial Harbinger (1850) were (1) Scripture as the sole authority,
(2) Christ as Messiah and Savior, (3) the ancient church order, (4) the

authority of the Messiah and apostles, as opposed to the Old Testament, and (5) cooperation among the churches. The ancient order entailed congregational independence, believer's baptism by immersion, weekly observation of the Lord's Supper, teaching elders and traveling nonsalaried evangelists. Theological formulations not found in Scripture (e.g., Calvinism, Arminianism, trinitarianism and unitarianism) were to be avoided. The proponents were strongly anticreedal, arguing that creeds generated schisms in the body of Christ. John Locke and the Scottish Enlightenment deeply influenced the leaders, who opposed unusual manifestations of the Holy Spirit in any form. Early preachers castigated the Westminster Confession for its distinctive Calvinistic tendencies and "metaphysical" language but agreed with about 80 percent of the conclusions, even though they did not admit as much.

The controversies leading to the 1906 separation were over state and national mission societies and over musical instruments in worship; the Churches of Christ were opposed to both practices. The Civil War added to the cultural aspects of the division. The Disciples tended to become more ecumenical, while the Churches of Christ saw themselves as outsiders both to American religion and society, controverting Christian history beyond New Testament times. Leaders among the Churches of Christ were Tolbert Fanning and David Lipscomb of Nashville, Tennessee, and Austin McGary of Austin, Texas.

Small factions have occurred over issues such as plural Communion cups, premillennialism and the disbursement of church funds to parachurch ministries. Lectureships, journals and universities stimulate cohesiveness. Leaders now tend to be more grace-oriented than in former times. There are over 15,000 autonomous congregations making up the Churches of Christ, with a membership of over 1,500,000. Eighty per cent of them live two hundred miles on either side of a line drawn from Chattanooga, Tennessee, to El Paso, Texas.

Conservative Baptist Association of America. An association of approximately 1,200 Baptist churches, chiefly in the northern and western areas of the U.S. Organized in Atlantic City, New Jersey, in 1947, the association is closely allied with the Conservative Baptist Foreign Mission Society; the Conservative Baptist Home Mission Society; Southwestern Bible College in Phoenix, Arizona; and three theological seminaries: Denver Seminary, Western Seminary and Eastern Conservative Baptist Seminary. The seven organizations constitute the Conservative Baptist movement. Total membership of the 1,200 churches in the association is approximately 200,000, but thousands more in other congregations, providing financial support for the missions and schools, add to the total strength of the movement.

Conservative Baptists prefer to speak of their *movement* rather than their *denomination* because the CBA creates only a loose affiliation for its churches. Unlike most denominations, it has no unified budget for its cooperating agencies. Each of the schools and mission societies has its own budget and board of directors. Structurally, then, Conservative Baptists operate more as cooperating interdenominational agencies than as a traditional denomination.

The association emerged from the fundamentalist-modernist controversy within the Northern (now *American) Baptist denomination. As early as 1921 conservative pastors within the convention attempted to establish doctrinal standards for the missionary agencies of the Northern Baptist Convention. But several votes at annual conventions (1922-1925) proved fruitless. Then, in 1943, after renewed but unsuccessful attempts to create theological tests for the Northern Baptist missionary program, several hundred conservative churches formed the Conservative Baptist Foreign Mission Society. Pastor Richard Beal at the First Baptist Church of Tucson, Arizona, and Pastor Albert Johnson at Hinson Baptist Church in Portland, Oregon, assumed the leadership in this action.

The conservative association of churches was organized when it became apparent, at the Northern Baptist Convention meeting at Grand Rapids, Michigan (1946), that the older convention would not tolerate a competing missionary agency within its structures. In the following years hundreds of Northern Baptist churches left their national convention to join the conservatives. In Minnesota and Arizona, conservatives even captured the state conventions of the denomination.

Conservative Baptist agencies grew rapidly during the first fifteen years of independent ministry, but in the late 1950s internal conflict developed over acceptable affiliations outside the movement. The vast majority of Conservative Baptist churches cooperated with other denominations and parachurch agencies in the National Association of Evangelicals, and specifically with the Billy Graham Association. A militant minority within Conservative Baptist circles, however, insisted that such cooperation was dangerous and to be avoided. These were the fundamentalists within Conservative Baptist circles. After seven years of intense debate over separation, the militant minority, consisting of about 200 churches, found a new home in fundamentalistic circles.

1501 W. Mineral Ave., Suite B
Littleton, CO 80120
Phone: (888) 627-1995; Fax: (720) 283-3333
Website: www.cbamerica.org

Conservative Congregational Christian Conference. An evangelical association of Congregational churches. This group of churches and ministers was organized in 1948 in order to provide a fellowship for evangelical churches and ministers who did not wish to become a part of the emerging *United Church of Christ, which brought together the General Council of Congregational and Christian Churches and the Evangelical and Reformed Church (1957).

The Conservative Congregational Christian Conference arose out of an earlier fellowship that was formed in 1945 to maintain a biblical witness within the General Council of Congregational and Christian Churches. This fellowship itself had developed out of an informal association of evangelicals that had existed within the regular Congregational denomination since the 1930s.

The Conference describes itself as a "fellowship of churches" and affirms its commitment to five principles in Congregationalism: (1) the necessity of a regenerate church membership, (2) the authority of the Holy Scriptures, (3) the lordship of Christ, (4) the autonomy of the local church, and (5) the voluntary fellowship of believers. It subscribes to a seven-article statement of faith. In recent years a number of evangelical Bible or community churches with congregational polity have joined the Conference, and as of 2001 there were 256 churches and a total membership of approximately 40,000.

7582 Currell Blvd., Suite 108
St. Paul, MN 55125

Phone: (651) 739-1474; Fax: (651) 739-0750
Website: www.ccccusa.org

Convention of Atlantic Baptist Churches. *See* Canadian Baptist Ministries.

Cumberland Presbyterian Church. Presbyterian denomination with churches predominantly in the South and West. An outgrowth of the frontier revivals of 1800 in Kentucky, this denomination originated on February 4, 1810, in Dickson County, Tennessee, with the formation of an independent Cumberland Presbytery by Finis Ewing, Samuel King and Samuel McAdow. This followed a lengthy controversy between the Cumberland Presbytery and the Presbyterian Church in the U.S.A. over subscription to the Westminster Confession's teaching on predestination, educational requirements for ministers and the extent of synodical authority over presbyteries.

The church enjoyed rapid growth on the frontier with the establishing of the Cumberland Synod in 1813 and the formation of a General Assembly in 1829. Growing fivefold between 1835 and 1860, the predominantly rural denomination established congregations from Pennsylvania to California. The Civil War did not result in a formal split. Following the revision by the Presbyterian Church in the U.S.A. of the Westminster Confession's teaching on divine sovereignty, a merger of the two denominations was approved in 1906. A continuing Cumberland Presbyterian Church was perpetuated, however, by a sizable minority that feared that doctrinal harmony between the two churches had not been achieved.

Standing self-consciously between Calvinism and Arminianism, Cumberland Presbyterians have held to a "medium theology" that affirms an unlimited atonement, universal grace, conditional election, the eternal security of the believer and the salvation of all children dying in infancy. The denomination lists 784 churches with a membership of 85,427. It supports Bethel College in McKenzie, Tennessee, and Memphis Theological Seminary. Close ties are maintained with the predominantly African American Second Cumberland Presbyterian Church, which subscribes to the Cumberland Presbyterian confessional standards.

1978 Union Avenue
Memphis, TN 38104
Phone: (901) 276-4572; Fax: (901) 272-3913
Website: www.cumberland.org

D

Doukhobors (Dukhobors). A mystical, communal Christian sect
with Ukrainian origins. Derived from *Dukhobortsy*, Russian for
"spirit wrestlers," the word was first applied in a pejorative sense
and later adopted by a mystical, pacifist, communal sect of Christians appearing around 1740 in the Kneiper River region of Ukraine.
Dissenting from the Orthodox Church, they taught that the "inner
light" or voice of God, what they also identified as the "Christ
Spirit," inhabited all things and persons. Hence, they denied the authority of the church, took an anarchist position toward government, embraced pacifism and eventually became vegetarians.

Doukhobors reject the authority of the Bible, revere Christ as a
sinless person and recognize God as present in fullest power in
other persons. They accept the Ten Commandments but hold that if
individuals follow their inner light, law and secular government are
unnecessary. Doukhobors are a communal society, worshiping in
meetings called *sobranyas*. Their only symbols are salt, water and
bread. Psalms, meditations and hymns, orally transmitted in the
"Living Book," transmit their doctrine, history and culture. Doukhobor leaders are revered as persons having a "magnified" spark of
the Divine.

In 1898, with the assistance of Count Leo Tolstoy and English
Quakers, 8,000 Doukhobors immigrated to Canada. Known as the
Christian Community of Universal Brotherhood, most settled in
communities in Saskatchewan on land received as individual home-
steads under the Dominion Lands Act (1873). In 1908 a majority
moved to the Kootenays in British Columbia, where 6,000 settled
communally on property privately purchased.

Assimilationist pressures in Canada gave rise early on to the ac-
commodationist Independent Doukhobors. In 1902 a reactionary
splinter group of radical millennarians arose called "The Sons of
Freedom." In protest of state-imposed education and taxation, this

group has occasionally resorted to arson, bombing and parading naked. Their indebtedness led the government of British Columbia to foreclose on their land in 1939. Since World War II, violence and civil disobedience by a small minority have led to unwarranted prejudice against law-abiding Doukhobors.

In 2000 there were an estimated 34,000 Doukhobor descendants, half of whom continue to speak Russian and remain religiously active.

Union of Spiritual Communities of Christ
Box 760
Grand Forks, BC V0H 1H0
Phone: (250) 442-8252; Fax: (250) 442-3433
Website: www.doukhobors-homepage.com

Dutch Reformed. *See* Reformed Church in America.

E

Episcopal Church. *See* Protestant Episcopal Church in the U.S.A.

Evangelical Covenant Church of America. A Free Church denomination. Founded in Chicago in 1885 as the Swedish Evangelical Mission Covenant of America, the Evangelical Covenant Church of America traces its roots back to the pietistic revivals in eighteenth- and nineteenth-century Sweden. Dissatisfied with what they viewed as the formalism and lack of spiritual warmth of the state Lutheran Church of Sweden, groups of "mission friends" began to meet in conventicles in which leaders would direct small groups in prayer, singing and explication of Scripture. After immigration to America, the connections with the Lutheran Church became more and more tenuous, until finally on February 20, 1885, the new denomination was formed.

Rather than formulate a new creed, the founders of the church determined that the final authority of Scripture, along with affirmations of the historic creeds of the church, particularly the Apostles' Creed, would define the group. The Evangelical Covenant Church of America has been described as evangelical, but not exclusive; biblical, but not doctrinaire; traditional, but not rigid; and congregational, but not independent. The Reformation doctrine of justification by grace through faith has been regarded as fundamental to the dual tasks of evangelism and Christian nurture.

The church is governed by the annual meeting of ministers and laypersons who serve as delegates from the churches. An executive board elected by the annual meeting implements its decisions. There are eleven geographical districts governed by superintendents who, among other duties, guide local churches in their calling of ministers.

The headquarters of the denomination are in Chicago, where also the Swedish Covenant Hospital School of Nursing and North Park University and Theological Seminary are located. The Evangelical Covenant Church also supports a Bible institute in Canada and Minnehaha Academy in Minneapolis. Mission fields are in Africa, Alaska, China, Ecuador, Colombia, Japan, Mexico and Thailand. As of 2000, the church had 101,003 members in 800 churches.

5101 N. Francisco Ave.
Chicago, IL 60625
Phone: (773) 784-3000; Fax: (773) 784-4366
Website: www.covchurch.org

Evangelical Free Church of America. An evangelical denomination with roots in the Scandinavian Free Church movement. Born out of revival among the scattered immigrants who had left the Lutheran State Church in Scandinavia to come to America, the denomination dates officially to a conference of free churches held in Boone, Iowa, in 1884. In 1950 the Evangelical Free Church of America (Swedish) and the Evangelical Free Church Association (Norwegian-Danish) merged into the present body, The Evangelical Free Church of America (EFCA).

Committed to the absolute authority of the Scriptures and the premillennial and imminent return of the Lord, the EFCA statement of faith clearly enunciates the cardinal doctrines of the church but allows latitude in what it regards as "non-essentials to salvation," such as Calvinism and Arminianism, baptism, spiritual gifts and eschatological details compatible with premillennialism. The term *Free* indicates a congregational form of government wherein individual churches hold title to property as well as decide and govern their own affairs.

In the early 2000s there were approximately 1,200 Evangelical Free Church congregations in the U.S. and Canada with an active membership of 140,000. The U.S. and Canadian bodies maintain a fraternal relationship, sharing one overseas mission board overseeing over 400 missionaries on fourteen foreign fields. The denomination operates Trinity Evangelical Divinity School and Trinity International University in Deerfield, Illinois, as well as Trinity Western University in Langley, British Columbia.

901 East 78th Street
Minneapolis, MN 55420-1300
Phone: (952) 854-1300; Fax: (800) 745-2202
Website: www.efca.org

Evangelical Friends International. An organization of evangelical *Friends (Quaker) churches. Formed in 1965, the Evangelical Friends Alliance united Friends who had been influenced by evangelicalism. In 1990 the Evangelical Friends Alliance restructured to become the Evangelical Friends International, with the North American Region representing the United States and Canada. Appealing to the evangelical roots of Quakers in the seventeenth century, they include the Evangelical Friends Church, Eastern Division, which in the early nineteenth century came to include the Gurneyites, the evangelically inclined followers of Joseph John Gurney. The Gurneyites eventually adopted revivalistic methods and the pastoral system of ministry rather than the traditional Quaker system of untrained and unsalaried itinerants. In the late nineteenth century they were influenced by the burgeoning Holiness Movement.

The Evangelical Friends have attracted evangelical congregations of Friends from across the U.S. and now consist of four regional yearly meetings or districts. The Evangelical Friends support Malone College in Canton, Ohio, an institution originally founded by Walter and Emma Malone in 1892 as the Christian Workers Training School. Evangelical Friends number approximately 36,760 (1995) in North America and more than 140,000 worldwide.

5350 Broadmoor Cir. NW
Canton, OH 44709
Phone: (330) 493-1660; Fax: (330) 493-0852
Website: www.alliancefriendschurch.org

Evangelical Lutheran Church in America. The largest Lutheran denomination in America. The Evangelical Lutheran Church in America (ELCA) was organized April 20-May 3, 1987, in Columbus, Ohio, and officially born on January 1, 1988. It represents the merger of three Lutheran bodies: the Lutheran Church in America, the American Lutheran Church and the Association of Evangelical Lutheran Churches.

The lineage of the Lutheran Church in America (LCA) reached back to Henry Melchior Muhlenberg, who arrived in Pennsylvania in 1742 and worked to gather Lutheran immigrants and to plant the Lutheran Church. Three early Lutheran synods, the General Synod (1820), the United Synod South (1863) and the General Council (1867), formed the United Lutheran Church in America (ULCA) in 1918.

Subsequently, the ULCA attracted the Slovak Zion Synod (in 1920), the Icelandic Synod (joined in 1940), the (Finnish) Suomi Synod and one of two Danish groups, the American Evangelical Lutheran Church. Larger than these was a group of Swedish heritage, a vital body called The Augustana Synod, whose merger with the ULCA in 1962 was the largest force behind the creation of the Lutheran Church in America out of the old ULCA and some other bodies. Much of the LCA's constituent strength was in the East, and when it merged to form the ELCA, it brought 2.9 million members.

The American Lutheran Church (ALC) arose out of nineteenth-century Lutheran immigrants to America who tended to stress a blend of confessionalism and pietism. In time these Lutherans formed various bodies, including three Germanic groups: the Evangelical Joint Synod of Ohio and Other States (1818), the Buffalo Synod (1845), and the Iowa Synod (1854). In 1930 these three bodies formed the original American Lutheran Church.

They were joined in 1960 by a group with Norwegian origins, the Evangelical Lutheran Church. This body had been formed in 1917 out of Hauge's Synod (1846), the Norwegian Synod (1853) and the United Norwegian Lutheran Church of America (1890). It brought nearly 2,700 congregations and 1.5 million members to the merger. The third member of the union of 1960 was the United Evangelical Lutheran Church, which was of Danish lineage. Founded in 1896, it brought 181 congregations and 70,000 members to the union of 1960.

A later addition to the ALC was the Lutheran Free Church, which did not join until 1963. It was formed in 1897. They added 88,500 members and 288 congregations to the ALC.

The ALC was strongest in the Upper Midwest, and when it merged to form the ELCA, it consisted of 2.3 million members.

The Association of Evangelical Lutheran Churches formed in 1974 when the majority of students and faculty at Concordia Seminary, St. Louis, walked away from the *Lutheran Church—Missouri Synod. The controversy centered around issues of biblical interpretation and authority as well as ecumenical relationships with other Lutheran and non-Lutheran denominations.

The ELCA has its central office in Chicago. The 5,099,877 members and 10,766 churches are divided into 65 geographical synods grouped into nine regions. It is a member of the Lutheran World Federation, the National Council of Churches and the World Council of Churches.

8765 W. Higgins Road
Chicago, IL 60631
Phone: (800) 638-3522; Fax: (773) 380-1465
Website: www.elca.org

Evangelical Lutheran Church in Canada. The largest Lutheran body in Canada. The Evangelical Lutheran Church in Canada (ELCC) is the product of a number of mergers, most of which took place in the U.S. Because Canadian Lutheranism has had close links with the U.S., both official and unofficial, these mergers were experienced north of the border as well.

The first phase of ELCC came into being in 1960 and had three components. The largest was the Canadian district of the American Lutheran Church, which was largely in Eastern Canada and predominantly of German origin. It had originally been part of the Ohio Synod, which was long known for its robust theological conservatism and its keen sense of Lutheran distinctiveness.

The next component, and almost as large, was the Canadian district of the Evangelical Lutheran Church, which existed in Western Canada. This body was primarily Norwegian and represented the powerful evangelical movement that had developed in the homeland during the nineteenth century. While professing full loyalty to the Lutheran confessions and form of worship, there was a great deal of active lay involvement; prayer meetings and evangelistic services were commonplace, and Christian discipline frequently expressed itself most visibly in total abstinence from alcoholic beverage and the shunning of dancing. This segment brought a developed infrastructure, with a Bible college, a junior college and a seminary.

The smallest component was the Canadian section of the Danish United Evangelical Lutheran Church.

Together these became the Canadian district of the American Lutheran Church, which was known as the Evangelical Lutheran Church of Canada.

The second phase of ELCC came into operation when it became autonomous in 1967. The third phase occurred in 1985, when the Evangelical Lutheran Church of Canada joined with the Canadian district of the Lutheran Church in America, retaining autonomy and being known as the Evangelical Lutheran Church in Canada. As of 1998 baptized membership was 193,915.

302-393 Portage Avenue
Winnipeg, Manitoba R3B 3H6
Phone: (888) 786-6707
Website: www.elcic.ca

Evangelical Mennonite Brethren Conference. *See* Fellowship of Evangelical Bible Churches.

Evangelical Presbyterian Church. A new Presbyterian denomination. The formation of the Evangelical Presbyterian Church was precipitated by the apparent theological liberalism within the (northern) United Presbyterian Church in the United States of America and the (southern) Presbyterian Church in the U.S. When these two denominations began discussing a merger, eventually leading to the *Presbyterian Church (U.S.A.) in 1983, evangelical pastors and churches within the two denominations began exploring other options. Some chose to join the more conservative *Presbyterian Church in America (PCA). Others, though, felt that the PCA was theologically too restrictive. Thus in 1981 twelve churches birthed a new denomination: the Evangelical Presbyterian Church (EPC).

Taking the Westminster Confession as its basis of faith, the EPC identifies itself as "Presbyterian in government, Reformed in theology and Evangelical in spirit." Firm in its stand on the authority of Scripture and the traditional tenets of the Reformed faith, it nevertheless, believes that in nonessential matters there is room for freedom in belief and practice among Christians. Thus, for example, whether or not to have women officers or accept women pastors is up to individual congregations. The church is active in missionary outreach in twenty countries and has established a presbytery in Argentina.

The EPC comprises approximately 191 churches in 8 presbyteries, with a total membership of nearly 75,000.

29140 Buckingham Avenue, Suite 5
Livonia, MI 48154
Phone: (734) 261-2001; Fax: (734) 261-3282
Website: www.epc.org

F

Family, The. A group arising from the Jesus Movement of the 1960s. Founded in 1968 by David Berg in southern California, the movement has been known as Teens for Christ, Revolution for Jesus, Children of God, the Family of Love and now The Family. It emerged during the Jesus Movement era and soon became identified as the most radical of the Christian hippie groups.

Preaching an apocalyptic gospel and attacking the established institutions of conventional America, especially the church, Berg became known to his youthful followers as God's "End-Time Prophet." Communal in nature, the group is organized into colonies and has spread throughout the world. It has appealed to thousands of young people through its music, its sense of family and its unique form of mission.

Teaching as well as practical directives of all types were communicated to "disciples" via numerous "Mo Letters" from Berg, who became increasingly mysterious and reclusive. Many of the Mo Letters also revealed the unorthodox practices Berg was preoccupied with.

The Family is an example of extremism within the Jesus Movement that emerged from the context of rapid social and cultural

change characterizing American society in the 1960s.
    Website: www.thefamily.org

Fellowship of Evangelical Bible Churches. Formerly Evangelical
Mennonite Brethren Conference, the Fellowship of Evangelical Bible Churches (FEBC) was organized in 1889 as a schism among
Mennonites who emigrated from Russia to the U.S. in the 1870s.
Led by Isaac Peters of Henderson, Nebraska, and Aaron Wall of
Mountain Lake, Minnesota, the conference was a product of pietist and evangelical influences within traditional Mennonite
communities. An emphasis on individual morality and personal
salvation, coupled with openness to Sunday school, evangelistic
meetings and foreign missions, typified the conference from its
beginning. In recent years the conference has identified more
closely with its pietist/evangelical heritage than its Mennonite
doctrinal roots, to the point that it dropped the word Mennonite
from its name in 1987.
    The current name is the conference's fourth. Begun as the Con-
ference of United Mennonite Brethren of North America, it changed
its name in 1917 to the Defenseless Mennonite Brethren in Christ of
North America. In 1937 it became known as the Evangelical Mennonite Brethren Conference. From 1953 to 1962 the FEBC was loosely
affiliated with the Evangelical Mennonite Church through The Conference of Evangelical Mennonites. Membership is roughly 4,000 in
forty-one congregations in North America (1998). FEBC headquarters are in Omaha, Nebraska.
    3339 N. 109th Plz.
    Omaha, NE 68164
    Phone: (402) 965-3860; Fax: (402) 965-3871
    Website: www.members.aol.com/febcoma

Fellowship of Grace Brethren Churches. A conservative Brethren denomination. Although related to other evangelicals and
fundamentalists, the Grace Brethren differ from them in their emphasis on a peculiar observance of the Lord's Supper that includes the love feast and the service of foot washing. Other distinctive practices include anointing the sick with oil (according to
James 5) and refraining from amusements considered to be

worldly. The Brethren also practice adult baptism by triple forward immersion.

The Grace Brethren grew from a division that occurred at Ashland College and Seminary in 1937. As a result of this controversy, they emphasize congregational church government. Despite this local autonomy, the churches maintain a close relationship through annual district and national conferences where both lay and ministerial delegates vote on issues that concern the membership. There are also independent corporations that manage cooperative endeavors such as Home Missions, Foreign Missions and Grace Theological Seminary and College (Winona Lake, Indiana).

The church is characterized by a conservative social and political outlook and a sincere desire to share the gospel with unbelievers. This has led to an emphasis on missions both at home and abroad. A life of service to God in active Christian work is constantly presented to young people. As the church has grown, it has attracted many members from other traditions, and this has resulted in a decline in certain historical Brethren attitudes such as refusing to bear arms, take oaths and engage in lawsuits. In 1997 the group had a membership of 30,371 in over 260 congregations, most heavily concentrated in California, Ohio and Pennsylvania.

P.O. Box 386
Winona Lake, IN 46590
Phone: (574) 269-1269; Fax: (419) 844-6205
Website: www.fgbc.org

Free Methodist Church of North America. The Free Methodist Church of North America was founded in 1860 by the union of two unsuccessful reform movements in the Methodist Episcopal Church (*see* United Methodist Church). Laity expelled from a local church in Illinois under the leadership of J. W. Redfield were joined by ministers expelled from the Genessee annual conference in New York under the leadership of Benjamin T. Roberts. The group added the word *Free* to its name to show that it stood for free pews, freedom for the slaves and freedom in worship. Its doctrine and government were like the Methodist Church except that it expressly taught the possibility of entire sanctification and included an equal number of lay and ministerial representatives in every

decision-making body. Today the church remains close to its theological roots and supports a vigorous missions program. In 2001
there were 978 churches and over 61,000 members in the U.S., with
at least as many members in other countries. The denominational
headquarters are in Winona Lake, Indiana.

P.O. Box 535002
Indianapolis, IN 46253-5002
Phone: (800) 342-5531 or (317) 244-3660
Website: www.freemethodistchurch.org

Free Will Baptists. Formed in the eighteenth century in opposition
to Calvinist predestination among Regular Baptists, Free Will Baptists arose in this country from two streams. Paul Palmer formed
General Baptist churches in North Carolina in the 1720s. These
churches held a doctrine of "free will," that is, freedom of any to believe in Christ, as opposed to the Calvinist doctrine of predestination of the "elect" to salvation. In time most of these early "Freewillers" succumbed to intense proselytism of the Regular (Calvinist)
churches of the Philadelphia Baptist Association.

In 1780 another stream of Free Will Baptists arose in New England, led by Benjamin Randall. Converted in George Whitefield's revivals, Randall joined the Baptists in 1776 but broke with them in
1779 over predestination. In 1780 he formed a church of seven members at New Durham, New Hampshire. In time the Calvinism of
Regular Baptists moderated, diminishing the justification for Free
Will Baptists. In 1911 most Freewillers in the North merged into the
Northern Baptist Convention.

Remnants of the Palmer and Randall lines reestablished contact,
and in 1935 representatives from both groups met in Nashville, Tennessee, to form the National Association of Free Will Baptists
(NAFWB). They adopted a confession of faith in 1935 and established a college in Nashville in 1942. The Free Will Baptists are distinguished from other Baptists by their intense conservatism, centralized organizational structure and the practice of footwashing. In
2001 the NAFWB reported 197,919 members in 2,470 churches. The
United American Free Will Baptist Church (1867) and the General
Conference of Original Free Will Baptists (1962) represent smaller
groups with similar emphases.

P.O. Box 5002
Antioch, TN 37011-5002
Phone: (877) 767-7659 or (615) 731-6812
Website: www.nafwb.org

Friends (Quakers). *See* Evangelical Friends International; Friends General Conference; Religious Society of Friends (Quakers).

Friends General Conference (Hicksites). A branch of the *Religious Society of Friends. Hicksites derive their designation from the Long Island farmer and Quaker minister Elias Hicks. Earlier Quakers had used *Light* as a term synonymous with the Holy Spirit. With Hicks, the Light, as the autonomous and natural reason of the common laboring man, was exalted to primary authority. Among those views that Hicks found unreasonable was Christ's substitutionary death on the cross and his physical resurrection. Hicks also opposed missions, Bible societies, public schools, cooperative charitable and reform activities and industrial developments such as the Erie Canal.

Hicks led a schism among American Quakers that began in Philadelphia in 1827-1828. Modern Hicksites compose the Friends General Conference with a membership of approximately 32,000 in fourteen Annual Meetings. They maintain the traditional silent worship service but have abandoned any sort of designation of those who are especially called to public ministry.

1216 Arch St. #2B
Philadelphia, PA 19107
Phone: (215) 561-1700; Fax: (215) 561-0759
Website: www.fgcquaker.org

Fundamental Baptist Fellowship. A movement of separatist Baptist churches. In 1921 a group that came to be called the "Fundamentalist Fellowship" sought to rid Northern Baptist Convention (*see* American Baptist Churches in the U.S.A.) schools of liberal teachers. Meeting prior to the national conference of the Convention, they planned a strategy for imposing their views on the denomination as a whole. To this end they prepared a confession of faith known as The Goodchild Confession, based on the Philadelphia and New Hampshire Confessions. Their plans were shattered, however, by alternate committee reports and parliamentary maneuvers. In 1922 the denomination affirmed the New Testament as their only rule of faith in order to avert the adoption of a fundamentalist statement. Fundamentalists could muster only one-third of the voting participants for their doctrinal standard.

The Fundamentalist Fellowship never again had the opportunity to capture the Convention or put their policies into effect. Several smaller groups emerged from the Convention in the late 1920s, but the Fundamentalist Fellowship itself stayed within the denomination until the 1940s. In 1943 the fundamentalists, in protest of the policies of the Convention's foreign mission society, organized the Conservative Baptist Foreign Mission Society and laid the foundation for the *Conservative Baptist movement. A separatistic wing among the conservatives continued the critical influence of the Fundamentalist Fellowship until 1965 when it withdrew and adopted the name Fundamental Baptist Fellowship.

500 West Lee Road
Taylors, SC 29687
Phone: (800) 376-6856
Website: www.fbf-nc.org

G

General Association of Regular Baptist Churches. An association of fundamentalist Baptist churches. The General Association of Regular Baptist Churches (GARBC) was founded at the final meeting of the Baptist Bible Union in May 1932. The objectives of the GARBC were to (1) create an association of churches rather than a convention, (2) uphold the conservative Baptist New Hampshire Confession of Faith (1833) with a revised premillennial stance in the article on eschatology, and (3) work separately from the Northern Baptist Convention (*see* American Baptist Churches in the U.S.A.), promote missionary spirit, and assist churches in securing fundamentalist pastors.

The GARBC early came under the guiding influence of Robert T. Ketcham (1889-1978), who was elected vice president (1933), president (1934) and editor of *The Baptist Bulletin* (1938). He served as national representative from 1948 to 1960. In 1934 a council of fourteen (enlarged to eighteen in 1972) elected delegates from Association churches was established to carry out directives voted on by the churches at the annual meeting. At this same time the GARBC adopted a policy concerning approval of education and mission organizations. Each organization seeking approval must submit an annual request for approval, thereby allowing the GARBC opportunity to withdraw approval from those organizations not meeting GARBC standards. Today the GARBC approves seven colleges and seminaries, five mission agencies and several social programs. The Regular Baptist Press was begun in 1950 to carry out the publication needs of the GARBC, particularly *The Baptist Bulletin*.

Theologically, the issues of separation and eschatology have been distinctive of the GARBC. Regarding separation, the Association advocates "obedience to the Biblical commands to separate ourselves unto God from worldliness and ecclesiastical apostasy" (2 Cor 6:17; Rom 16:17). On the issue of eschatology, the GARBC believes in the premillennial return of Christ, rapture of the church, the great tribulation and Christ's establishment of the millennial kingdom (1 Thess 4:13-18; Dan 9:25-27; Rev 20).

In the early 2000s the GARBC had 1,417 fellowshiping churches with a total membership of 132,522.

1300 N. Meacham Rd.
Schaumburg, IL 60173-4806
Phone: (888) 588-1600 or (847) 843-1600
Website: www.garbc.org

General Baptists. Those Baptists named for their adherence to the Arminian doctrine of general atonement, which claims that Christ died for all persons. Their first church was gathered by John Smyth in 1608/1609 and Separatists who had followed him in exile to Amsterdam. When Smyth sought closer ties with local Mennonites, Thomas Helwys led a schismatic group to Spitalfields (London), where they planted the first Baptist church in England (1612). Growing to forty-seven churches by 1650, General Baptists formed a national general assembly by 1654 and issued the Standard Confession (1660) and the Orthodox Creed (1678). Their earliest American churches resulted from schisms in Particular-General churches: Providence (1652), Newport (1665) and Swansea (c. 1680). Also known as Six-Principle Baptists, they held Arminian doctrine, opposed singing in worship and required hands to be laid upon new converts.

General Baptists formed what is perhaps the first (temporary) Baptist association in America (c. 1670) and the first Baptist churches in New York (1714), Virginia (1714) and North Carolina (1727). Suffering from doctrinal ambiguity, diminishing evangelism, hesitancy to organize, untrained ministers and proselytizing by Regular Baptists, they were almost extinct by 1800. A new movement, led by Benoni Stinson after 1822, culminated in formation of the General Association of General Baptists (1870). With headquarters at Poplar Bluff, Missouri, it covers sixteen Midwestern states, supports Oakland City (Indiana) College and maintains boards for home and foreign missions, ministers' aid, publications, education and women's work. In 2002 there were 713 American churches with 70,000 members, and 14,820 members overseas.

100 Stinson Drive
Poplar Bluff, MO 63901
Phone: (573) 785-7746
Website: www.generalbaptists.com

General Conference Mennonite Church. The second-largest organized body of Mennonites in North America. The General Conference Mennonite Church (GCMC) was organized in 1860 as an agency for Mennonite denominational unity, mission work, Christian education and publication. Its progressive agenda attracted Mennonite congregations who were becoming Americanized and wanted to move beyond Mennonite traditionalism, legalism and separation from the world. The Conference holds to traditional Anabaptist-Mennonite teachings, including nonresistance. It does not have an official creed and follows a congregational polity.

The GCMC embraces greater cultural variety than other Mennonite bodies. The first congregations were of Swiss and south-German background, located in Pennsylvania and the Midwest. In the 1870s, 1920s and 1940s, numerous congregations of immigrants of Dutch extraction who had immigrated to Russia and Eastern Europe and then to the U.S. joined the Conference. Most of the later immigrants came to Canada, where about 43 percent of the Conference's membership lives. In recent decades the congregations have undergone a major shift from rural areas to small towns and to urban centers.

Early GCMC mission work produced congregations in India, China and among the Cheyenne, Arapahoe and Hopi Indians. A major expansion in mission after World War II led to additional work in Japan, Taiwan, Colombia and in other countries of Africa and Latin America. The GCMC has contributed to the international relief and service ministries of the Mennonite Central Committee, as well as to institutions for health care for the aged, to mental health facilities, church camping, mutual aid, disaster service and related activities.

The GCMC seminary is in Elkhart, Indiana. The Conference is also indirectly related to eight Bible institutes and to colleges in Bluffton, Ohio; North Newton, Kansas; Winnipeg, Manitoba; and Waterloo, Ontario. The publishing arm of the Conference is Faith and Life Press, Newton, Kansas, where the denominational headquarters are also located. In 1997 the total number of congregations in the GCMC stood at 521, with 67,353 members.

4812 E. Butler Ave.
Fresno, CA 93727
Phone: (209) 452-1713; Fax: (209) 452-1752

General Conference of Mennonite Brethren Churches of North America. A Mennonite denomination growing out of Mennonite immigrants from Russia and Crimea. Between 1874 and 1884 it is estimated that approximately 18,000 Mennonites immigrated from Russia to North America. Among these immigrants were some 200 families affiliated with the Mennonite Brethren Church, a group founded in Russia in 1860, who settled in Kansas, Nebraska, Minnesota and the Dakota Territory. These congregations organized themselves as a General Conference in 1879. In 1909 the General Conference was subdivided into three district conferences. Today there are five district conferences in sixteen states and six provincial conferences in seven Canadian provinces. In 1996 membership stood at 82,130 in 360 churches. In 1960 the Krimmer Mennonite Brethren Conference merged with the Mennonite Brethren, adding approximately 1,600 members to the Conference roles.

The Conference supports an extensive foreign mission program, with missionaries in more than twenty countries. The Conference seminary is Mennonite Brethren Biblical Seminary in Fresno, California, and several other colleges and Bible institutes are operated by various district conferences. The Mennonite Brethren Conference is a member of the National Association of Evangelicals and Mennonite Central Committee.

3-169 Riverton Ave.
Winnipeg, Manitoba R2L 2E5
Phone: (204) 669-6575; Fax: (204) 654-1865
Website: www.mbconf.ca

General Synod of the Associate Reformed Presbyterian Church. A small Presbyterian denomination. Derived mainly from Scottish seceder heritage, the Associate Reformed Presbyterian Church (ARPC) members immigrated to the American colonies in the 1700s. The seceders formed the ARPC in 1782 through union with Reformed, or covenanting, Presbyterians. The new church grew to establish four synods by 1803, and in 1804 the first general synod was formed. Controversies over exclusive psalm-singing, closed Communion and church government led eventually to synodical defections and to the merger that began the United Presbyterian Church in 1858. Only the Synod of the South and a very small Associate Church minority remained outside the union.

The Synod of the South continued the heritage of the ARPC. It grew slowly due to internal conflict and migration of its antislavery members to the North. In 1837 Erskine Seminary was established, in part to train pastors. Erskine College was founded in 1839. Growth was stabilized, in part due to home mission emphases sometimes involving a colonizing method whereby a part or the whole of a congregation would move to a new settlement. Known as the Associate Reformed Presbyterian Church since 1858, in 1935 the term *General Synod* was added (GS, ARPC).

Genuine piety, an increasing emphasis on local church government and allegiance to the Westminster standards—maintained with varying degrees of firmness—characterize the GS, ARPC. Exclusive psalm singing became optional in 1946. Statistics for 2002 indicated that the GS, ARPC had 266 churches and 35,379 members.

1 Cleveland St., Ste. 110
Greenville, SC 29601-3696
Phone: (864) 232-8297; Fax: (864) 271-3729
Website: www.arpsynod.org

Greek Orthodox Archdiocese of North and South America. The largest Orthodox jurisdiction in the U.S. The actual growth of Orthodox Christianity in the U.S. began to occur in the years following the American Civil War. Under the direction of Orthodox merchants, diplomats and immigrants of various ethnic backgrounds, early parishes were established in New Orleans in 1864, San Francisco in 1867 and New York City in 1870.

The growth in the number of parishes serving the specific needs of Greek Orthodox in America took place in the wake of the massive influx of immigrants from Greece and Asia Minor between 1880 and 1920. By this time there were about 150 parishes located throughout the U.S. These early parishes were served by priests who came to the U.S. with the approval of their ecclesiastical superiors either in the Patriarchate of Constantinople or in the Church of Greece. Throughout this early period there was no resident Greek Orthodox bishop to unify or to direct the parishes in accordance with canon law.

The Patriarchate of Constantinople affirmed its ecclesiastical authority over the Orthodox in America in 1908. In 1922 the Archdiocese of North and South America was canonically established, thereby sanctioning the earlier civil incorporation, and Archbishop Alexander (1876-1942) was elected as its first archbishop, with his see in New York. Other bishoprics were established in Chicago, Boston and San Francisco. While some ecclesial leaders may have envisioned a unified archdiocese uniting all Orthodox parishes in the Americas, the particular needs of the Greek immigrants precluded this possibility.

When Metropolitan Athenagoras of Kerkyera was elected as the new archbishop in 1930, his principal task was to bring unity to the Greek Orthodox in America. During his eighteen years as archbishop, Athenagoras succeeded in uniting the parishes and in establishing a college and theological school, an orphanage, a national church magazine and a national association of women known as the

Philoptochos Society. He also encouraged greater unity among all the Orthodox jurisdictions in America. Athenagoras was elected the Patriarch of Constantinople in 1948.

During the period from 1949 to 1958, when Archbishop Michael served as head of the Archdiocese, important demographic changes began to take place: new parishes were established in the suburbs, the majority of the members were now persons born and raised in the U.S., and not all were of Greek ethnic background. Reflecting these developments, there was a growing desire for a national youth organization, church-school programs and religious literature in the English language. There were also those who called for the greater use of English in liturgical services. This development, however, did not take place formally until the mid-1960s.

Known for his special interest in ecumenical relations and social concern, Archbishop Iakovos headed the Archdiocese from 1959 to 1996. In 1996 Archbishop Spyridon was appointed head of the Greek church. It now consists of more than 500 parishes and claims two million communicants throughout the U.S., Canada and Central and South America. In addition to the archdiocesan see, there are ten dioceses headed by a bishop. Clergy and lay representatives meet biannually. The entire Archdiocese is a province of the Patriarchate of Constantinople. As its exarch in the Americas, Spyridon also presides over the Standing Council of Canonical Orthodox Bishops, which brings together the presiding hierarchs from nine other Orthodox jurisdictions. The Archdiocese oversees Hellenic College and Holy Cross Greek Orthodox School of Theology in Brookline, Massachusetts. The Archdiocese is a major sponsor of missionary work in Africa, Korea and Indonesia.

8 East 79th Street
New York, NY 10021
Phone: (212) 570-3500; Fax: (212) 570-3569
Website: www.goarch.org

H

Hicksites. *See* Friends General Conference.

Holdeman Mennonites. *See* Church of God in Christ, Mennonite.

Hutterian Brethren (Hutterites). A communal form of sixteenth-century Anabaptism that has survived and flourishes in North America. Hutterite origins may be traced to Moravia, where persecuted Anabaptists from Switzerland and Tyrol found refuge in the mid-1520s. Jacob Wiedemann gathered these early pacifist dissenters into a fellowship at Austerlitz in 1528, where they practiced a "community of goods" (according to Acts 2:44-47). A few years later Jacob Hutter (martyred in 1536) reorganized the unstable and struggling group into the movement that still bears his name. Somewhat later Peter Riedemann published a Confession of Faith (1540), a statement that has since become the accepted authority for Hutterite faith and practice. Distinctive features of Hutterian life include believers' baptism, nonresistance, separation of church and state, distinctive dress and communitarian living.

The Hutterite colonies in Moravia experienced a "golden age" during the mid-sixteenth century but were harshly persecuted and suppressed by the Counter Reformation. A few refugees were able to remove to Hungary and Romania, and eventually further east to the Ukraine (1756). When privileges granted by the Tsarist government were withdrawn in 1870, three colonies immigrated to the U.S. from 1874 to 1877. Because of unfavorable treatment by the military during World War I, most of the Hutterites moved to Canada (1918), although many later returned to the U.S. In the late 1990s there were over 400 communities with about 42,800 members, primarily in the U.S. and Canada.

Website: www.hutterites.org (unofficial)

I

Independent Fundamental Churches of America. An organization of independent fundamentalist churches and agencies. The Independent Fundamental Churches of America (IFCA) began out of a desire to unite fundamentalists across denominational lines. Several leaders had been a part of the American Council of Undenominational Churches but wanted to create an organization for fundamentalists within denominations.

In 1930 thirty-nine men met with William McCarrell, pastor of the Cicero Bible Church, Cicero, Illinois. Others present were J. Oliver Buswell Jr., Martin R. DeHaan, Wendell P. Loveless, William L. Pettingill and John F. Walvoord. Out of this group there were twelve Congregationalists, three Presbyterians, nineteen Independents, one Baptist and four with no denominational identification. Together they began the IFCA.

The present bylaws state that the purpose is to unify those that have "separated from denominations which include unbelievers and liberal teachers" and to encourage one another in world evangelism. There are sixteen points to the doctrinal statement, including the verbal, plenary inspiration of the Bible; Christ's virgin birth, deity, sinless life, atoning death and bodily resurrection; and Christ's premillennial, pretribulational return. It also includes statements opposing ecumenism, ecumenical evangelism, neo-orthodoxy and neo-evangelicalism.

The group grew slowly at first and reported only 38 churches in 1935, with a membership of 550. Today there are 61,655 members in 659 churches, twenty-three church-extension organizations, seven schools, five camps and conferences, twenty home-mission agencies, three foreign-mission agencies and one Christian home.

P.O. Box 810
Grandville, MI 49468-0810
Phone: (800) 347-1640
Website: www.ifca.org

International Church of the Foursquare Gospel. Pentecostal denomination. The International Church of the Foursquare Gospel grew out of Pentecostal evangelist Aimee Semple McPherson's Angelus Temple in Los Angeles.

McPherson, a young widow and successful Pentecostal evangelist, arrived in California in 1918 with her two children, Roberta and Rolf. Though associated with the Assemblies of God, her ministry was largely interdenominational until she founded the Foursquare in 1927. In California she attracted thousands to her meetings, which, under her flamboyant leadership, offered salvation, prayer for the sick, baptism in the Holy Spirit, speaking in tongues and a concern for the needy.

In 1923 the 5,300-seat Angelus Temple was completed and a Bible school to train ministers and missionaries, Lighthouse International Foursquare Evangelism (L.I.F.E.), was opened in 1925. The church went on the air with its own radio station, and Angelus Temple became a dynamic center of Pentecostal worship and ministry.

The "Foursquare Gospel" was derived from the four-faced figures of Ezekiel 1, which McPherson reported seeing in a vision in 1921. The faces (a man, a lion, an ox and an eagle) were interpreted as the fourfold gospel of salvation, baptism in the Holy Spirit, divine healing and the Second Coming of Christ. These tenets placed the church in the mainstream of the Pentecostal movement. Yet the church holds to a progressive view of sanctification, rather than the Wesleyan perfectionism.

Church growth in the 1920s was spectacular but then leveled off until about 1970. The charismatic renewal in mainline denominations prompted further growth, and by 1985 the church had expanded to more than 1,200 local congregations. In 2002 the largest Foursquare church in the U.S. was the Church on the Way in Van Nuys, California (more than 6,000 members), pastored by Jack Hayford. Total church membership in 2002 was 235,852 in the U.S. The estimated attendance in the Foursquare Church worldwide now stands at 3,865,827 people. They worship in more than 35,000 congregations.

Foursquare is a charter member of the National Association of Evangelicals and the Pentecostal Fellowship of North America. The church was organized with an essentially episcopal polity.

P.O. Box 26902
Los Angeles, CA 90026-0176
Phone: (213) 989-4500
Website: www.foursquare.org

J

Jehovah's Witnesses. A religious body originating with Charles Taze Russell, also known as The Watchtower Bible and Tract Society of New York, Inc. The movement grew out of an independent Bible study started in Pittsburgh by Charles Taze Russell in 1870 and acquired its present name in 1956. Russell, who had privately studied Scripture for years and come to radical Adventist conclusions, soon became the group's pastor and in 1876 began the publication of a small magazine, *Zion's Watchtower*, which eventually became to-day's *Watchtower* (over 18 million copies published bimonthly in 106 languages). Russell's organization became the Zion's Watch Tower Tract Society in 1884, and in 1909 he moved its headquarters to Brooklyn, New York, where it has remained. The original theology of the movement was worked out by Russell in his seven-volume *Studies in the Scriptures* (1886-1917), which over the years has sold millions of copies. The final volume appeared a year after Russell's death and led to a schism in the organization.

Most of Russell's followers joined J. F. Rutherford, to form the Millennial Dawnists, who adopted the name Jehovah's Witnesses in 1931. A smaller group rejected Rutherford's leadership and became the Dawn Bible Student's Association and in the late 1980s had a membership of about 60,000. In the late 1990s the Jehovah's Witnesses proper reported around 990,000 members in the U.S. with over 11,000 in Canada.

Theologically, the Witnesses do not have a well-defined systematic theology and frequently change their teachings, though without official acknowledgment. In many respects, however, they resemble traditional Roman Catholicism rather than Protestantism because of their understanding of doctrinal and ecclesiastical authority, which is the key to their theology.

Russell's prophetic office was given official recognition as a result of challenges to his authority by dissident members in 1895. The prophetic office was later applied to Russell's successors, and to the leadership of the Witnesses collectively, to give the group a doctrinal stance almost identical to the magisterium of Roman Catholicism. The authority of the leadership is bound together by an understanding of progressive revelation whereby the leadership receives both direct revelation from God and an authoritative understanding of Scripture through their function as the "faithful and discreet slave," which is a prophetic class within the organization.

Theologically the Witnesses deny orthodox teachings about the person and work of Christ, arguing that Jesus was "a god" who died on a "torture stake" as a ransom to the devil. Their Christology is thus pseudo-Arian, emphasizing Jesus as the "Second Adam" who was essentially a perfect man. Baptism and the Lord's Supper are not sacraments. Baptism, by total immersion, is a "witness" to God that all members must undergo. In addition, there is a "baptism into Christ" (see Rev 7 and 14) which consecrates the 144,000 elect believers who will attain heavenly glory. The Lord's Supper is an annual feast that can only be fully participated in by those Witnesses who know themselves to be among the 144,000 who represent the totality of Christians who go to be with Christ. According to the society's statistics there were 9,601 of these "blessed" individuals alive in 1981. By contrast, most Witnesses have to be content with eternal life on earth.

Three other doctrines form an essential part of Witness doctrine and have brought them notoriety. First is their eschatology that has repeatedly proved false because of their habit of setting dates—Russell himself maintained that Christ had spiritually returned to earth in 1874 and would begin his visible reign in 1914. Second, their belief in the sacredness of life and refusal to imbibe blood in any form has led to a rejection of both military service and blood transfusions. Third, the preaching work whereby Witnesses are expected to proclaim their gospel as a means of obtaining salvation by works has made their presence known in many North American communities. In recent years the movement has been split by schisms and continual accusations of harsh treatment meted out to ex-members. During the 1930s and 1940s the Witnesses fought and won many court cases, forty-three in the U.S. Supreme Court, in the interest of their religious freedom.

25 Columbia Heights
Brooklyn, NY 11201-2483
Phone: (718) 560-5000; Fax: (718) 560-5619
Website: www.jw-media.org

L

Liberal Catholic Church. A religious movement with origins in Theosophy and founded in Great Britain. The Liberal Catholic Church was founded by James Ingall Wedgwood in London in 1916. In addition to Wedgwood, the church recognizes Charles W. Leadbeater as its cofounder. Its historical and theological roots can be traced to the Old Catholic Church, from which it emerged; the Anglican Church, with which its early leaders were formerly affiliated;

but most significantly the Theosophical Society, whose mystical tradition it adapted to Catholic ritual.

Congregations are generally quite small, and membership in America probably numbers no more than a few thousand. The church was established in the U.S. in 1919. In the 1940s a dispute arose between the presiding bishop of London and some American clergy. This resulted in a division of the church into the Liberal Catholic Church, Province of the U.S. (LCC), which remains close to the London church and its more Theosophical orientation (although the church has no formal ties with Theosophy), and the Liberal Catholic Church International (LCCI), which is theologically more orthodox.

Both churches affirm complete freedom of belief for their followers. Central to the theology of both are the sacraments and especially the Eucharist. Notable doctrinal positions of the LCC include belief in (1) the innate divinity of humanity; (2) reincarnation and denial of hell; (3) spiritual masters (saints), which spiritually interact with humanity; (4) Christ as divine messenger, historically manifested through others in addition to Jesus; and (5) the necessity of an exclusively male clergy. The LCCI, on the other hand, has dropped its Theosophical beliefs and requires that its clergy accept the "basic tenets of Catholic Christianity" (e.g., the Trinity and the Real Presence of the Lord in the Sacrament of the Altar). Both accept married and celibate clergy, both remarry divorced people, both are open to active homosexuals.

LCC	LCCI
1502 East Ojai Avenue	741 Cerro Gordo Ave.
Ojai, CA 93024	San Diego, CA 92102
Phone: (805) 646-5943	Phone and Fax: (619) 239-0637
Fax: (805) 646-2324	Website: www.liberalcatholic.org
Website: http://members.tripod	
.com/~LiberalCatholic/index.htm	

Lutheran Church—Missouri Synod. A large Lutheran denomination of German background. On April 26, 1847, a group of German-American pastors and their congregations organized the German Evangelical Lutheran Synod of Missouri, Ohio, and Other States. The word *German* was dropped from the name in World War I, and in its centennial year the official name became The Lutheran

Church—Missouri Synod (LCMS) with the "Missouri" recalling the original German-Lutheran immigrants who came to Perry County, Missouri, in 1839. The denominational headquarters, major seminary and publishing house are also located in St. Louis, Missouri.

The original immigrants included in the Missouri group had immigrated in 1838 under the leadership of Martin Stephan. Stephan and his group had left Saxony in protest against the rationalism that had infiltrated the German Lutheran church, as well as the Prussian Union which had forced a merger of Lutheran and Reformed churches. Congregations in Michigan and Indiana were founded by German Lutheran missionaries sent by the Franconian confessional Lutheran pastor Wilhelm Loehe. All of these groups had been influenced by conservative pietism as well as the revival of Lutheran confessionalism in early nineteenth-century Germany.

Under the leadership of its first two presidents, Carl F. W. Walther (president, 1847-1850; 1864-1878) and F. C. D. Wyneken (president, 1850-1864), the Synod developed a strong defense of its biblical theology, anchored in the sixteenth-century Lutheran confessions of the Book of Concord, and its congregational polity. This polity led to disputes with German Lutherans and with other German-American Lutherans, including the Buffalo Synod of Johannes A. A. Grabau and the Iowa Synod, founded by other disciples of Loehe.

These disputes and related doctrinal discussions led the Synod to arrange a series of free conferences (1856-1859) and colloquies (1866-1867), out of which came the organization of the Evangelical Lutheran Synodical Conference, an organization in which the Missouri Synod took the lead until its dissolution of the Conference in 1967. In its early years the Conference was rent by a dispute over predestination (1879-1883), in which the Missouri Synod, accused of "crypto-Calvinism," defended Luther's understanding of the unconditional election of believers to salvation.

Under Walther, Wyneken, H. C. Schwan (1819-1905; president, 1878-1899) and Franz Pieper (president, 1899-1911), the Synod trained pastors who organized German immigrants into congregations and created the largest single German Protestant denomination in North America.

In 1893 the LCMS began foreign mission work in India. Mission work in China, begun independently by a synodical college profes-

sor E. L. Arndt, was incorporated in the Synod's program in 1917.
Rapid expansion of foreign missions took place after World War II.
In 1987 the LCMS was involved in denominational or cooperative
mission outreach in thirty-five nations on four continents.

Two long-related churches, the Finnish-descended National
Evangelical Lutheran Church (organized 1898) and the former Slovak Evangelical Lutheran Church (organized 1902), were assimi-
lated into the LCMS in 1964 and 1971 respectively.

The LCMS has two seminaries: Concordia in St. Louis, Missouri
(founded 1839), and Concordia in Fort Wayne, Indiana (founded
1846), and more than a dozen liberal arts colleges.

In 1974 a majority of students and faculty at Concordia Seminary,
St. Louis, walked out and formed the Christ Seminary-Seminex and
the Association of Evangelical Lutheran Churches (AELC). The
group comprised 4 percent of the Synod's membership. In 1987 the
AELC merged with two larger Lutheran denominations to form the
*Evangelical Lutheran Church in America.

The LCMS continues its commitment to a strict interpretation of
the Lutheran confessions, a strong educational program at every
level and a firm commitment to evangelism and missions. In 2002
the membership numbered 2.5 million, making it the second-largest
Lutheran denomination in the U.S.

1333 S. Kirkwood Road
St. Louis, MO 63122-7295
Phone: (888) 643-5267
Website: www.lcms.org

M

Maronite Catholics. Eastern-rite Catholics with origins in northern
Syria. The Maronite Church traces its origins to the fourth century
and to the monk Maron (d. 423). Centuries later, a community of
Maronites grew up around the Monastery of Saint Maron on the
banks of the Orontes River in northern Syria. Seeking to escape from
the persecutions of the Caliphates of Damascus and Baghdad, Maronites sought refuge in the mountains of Lebanon. Although the
Maronite Church never rejected the primacy of the bishop of Rome,
communication between the two churches was interrupted for cen-

turies, and only after 1182 and the advent of the Crusaders was Roman recognition of the Maronite rite restored.

The Maronite Church is the only Eastern-rite Catholic church that does not have a parallel Orthodox hierarchy. The rite of the Maronite Church belongs to a group of Antiochene rites, and its liturgical language is West Syriac or Aramaic. The Maronites adopted more and more the use of Arabic as that language became the vernacular. Political and economic turmoil in the Middle East has caused the immigration of a large number of Maronites to the U.S. The original Eparchy [Diocese] of Saint Maron was located in Detroit, Michigan. In 1977 the see of the Eparchy was moved to Brooklyn, New York. In 1994 Pope John Paul II established two eparchies in the U.S. The Eparchy of Saint Maron of Brooklyn comprises the 38 parishes and missions along the Atlantic coast states. The Eparchy of Our Lady of Lebanon of Los Angeles comprises 31 parishes and missions in the Southern, Midwest and Western states.

Eparchy of Saint Maron of Brooklyn	Eparchy of Our Lady of Lebanon of Los Angeles
109 Remsen Street	1021 South Tenth St.
Brooklyn, NY 11201	St. Louis, MO 63104
Phone: (718) 237-9913	Phone: (314) 231-1021
Website: www.stmaron.org	Fax: (314) 231-1418
	Website: www.usamaronite.org

Melchite Greek Catholic Church. Eastern-rite Catholics arising out of the patriarchates of Alexandria, Antioch and Jerusalem. Melchites (from the Syriac, or Arabic, word for "king" or "emperor") were given this name by the anti-Chalcedonian party because they adhered to the Christological position of the Byzantine emperor after the Council of Chalcedon (451). Until the 1300s the Melchites used the Antiochene rite. In the countryside the liturgy was celebrated in West Syriac or Aramaic, and in the cities in Greek. With the advent of Islam, Arabic gradually replaced Syriac. In the course of the fourteenth century, the Byzantine rite replaced the Antiochene rite.

The Melchite faithful tried to preserve allegiance to both Rome and Constantinople. By 1724 renewed communication with Rome had resulted in the creation of a Catholic Melchite Church parallel to the Orthodox Melchite Church, although no formal written agreement of union was ever drawn up. The patriarch of Antioch, Maximos Mazloum (1833-1855), added the sees of Alexandria and Jerusalem to his title. Patriarch Maximos IV Sayegh (1947-1967) defended the traditions of the East in his patriarchate and at Vatican II in Rome. Many Melchite Catholics immigrated to North and South America at the beginning of the twentieth century and formed two eparchies (dioceses), in Newton, Massachusetts, and in Sao Paolo, Brazil. The Eparchy of Newton oversees 41 parishes in 18 states.

3 VFW Parkway
Roslindale, MA 02131
Phone: (617) 323-5242; Fax: (603) 644-2371
Website: www.melkite.org

Mennonite Church. As a North American body the Mennonite Church, frequently called the "Old" Mennonite Church (to be distinguished from Old Order Mennonites), goes back to colonial times and the first major Mennonite immigration to Pennsylvania in 1683. Many waves of immigrations, especially from Switzerland, South Germany and Alsace, brought Mennonites first of all to southeast Pennsylvania. Gradually, others came to Maryland, Virginia and the Carolinas, and later to Ontario, Ohio, Indiana, Illinois, Iowa and Kansas. Today Mennonites can be found in almost every province and state of Canada and the U.S.

After 1890 the spirit of evangelical revivalism and the missionary outreach of the Western world renewed Mennonite interests in urban as well as overseas missions. Mennonite interest in higher education also began about this time. From the 1890s to about 1950, a cultural conservatism developed that set the Mennonite Church apart culturally—in dress and other customs—from their contemporaries. This development contrasted with earlier Mennonites for whom simplicity in dress and life had meant avoiding extremes rather than wearing a peculiar garb. Both fundamentalism and liberalism also affected the church during the first half of the twentieth century.

The change from German to the English language and the acceptance of many new ideas eroded the strong sense of continuity with the mainstream of the Anabaptist-Mennonite tradition to the point that (Old) Mennonites were in danger of losing their historical rootedness. Hence the new quest for roots, begun in the 1920s at Goshen College (Indiana), was a necessary counterbalance in maintaining a Mennonite identity.

Since World War II, the once-rural Mennonites have become increasingly urbanized. The traditional stand of nonresistance was thoroughly tested by the violence and upheavals of the 1960s, and this time emerged substantially transformed, having taken into account the modern complexities of urbanized society.

Prior to 1860 there was no attempt to create a unified denominational structure for all North American Mennonites. But after the eastern Pennsylvania schism of 1847, "New Mennonites" came into being who in turn referred to the Franconia Conference of Mennonites as "Old Mennonites." In 1860 the "New Mennonites" helped to establish the denominational structure known as the *General Conference Mennonite Church. The term *Old Mennonites* was never an official term, although it was commonly used for purposes of identification. *Mennonite Church* was the unofficial designation prior to 1971, but since then it has become the official designation.

Today the Mennonite Church's structure includes a board of congregational ministries, of education, of missions, of mutual aid and a publication board. The Mennonite Church has a modified congregational polity. The congregation is the locus of authority, although congregations belong to conferences, which in turn relate to the Mennonite Church General Board. Conferences send delegates to the biennial Mennonite Church General Assembly, to which the General Board is responsible. The Mennonite Church is the oldest and largest of the several organized Mennonite groups in North America, with an adult membership of over 118,000 (with approximately 10 percent of that number in Canada and 90 percent in the U.S.).

500 S. Main St., P.O. Box 1245
Elkhart, IN 46515-1245
Phone: (574) 294-7523; Fax: (574) 293-1892
Website: www.mennonites.org

Moonies. *See* Unification Church.

Moravian Church in America. Popular name for two provinces of the *Unitas Fratrum* (Unity of the Brethren) in the U.S. and Canada. Founded by followers of John Hus in 1457, the movement was renewed under the patronage of Count Nicholas Ludwig von Zinzendorf in the 1720s. The first group of Moravians to settle in North America arrived in Savannah, Georgia, in 1735 under the leadership of Augustus G. Spangenberg. In 1740 the colony relocated to Pennsylvania and in 1741 founded a settlement at Bethlehem. Early Moravian ministers itinerated among the Germans living in Pennsylvania, and under the leadership of David Zeisberger carried out mission work among Native Americans.

The Moravians experienced little growth until German immigrations in the nineteenth century, which resulted in congregations founded in Wisconsin, New Jersey, Minnesota and North Dakota. In the twentieth century Moravians have founded churches in Florida; Arizona; California; Georgia; Washington, D.C.; and Ontario, Canada. Administratively, the churches are divided into two provinces with headquarters in Bethlehem, Pennsylvania, and Winston-Salem, North Carolina. In 2003 the Moravian Church reported 160 congregations and 50,000 members in 17 states and 2 provinces. The churches have adopted a conferential system of church government.

Moravian worship is semi-liturgical, with Scripture-based liturgies and services for the church year. Emphasis is placed on congregational singing and an extensive treasury of early-American Moravian anthems and sacred songs. Chorale hymnody is characteristic, although other hymns are freely used. Moravians are also known for their traditional Christmas Eve candle services, love feasts and Easter dawn services.

P.O. Box 1245
Bethlehem, PA 18016
Phone: (610) 867-0593; Fax: (610) 866-9223
Website: www.moravian.org

Mormons. *See* Church of Jesus Christ of Latter-day Saints.

N

National Association of Free Will Baptists. *See* Free Will Baptists.

National Baptists. Four predominantly African American Baptist denominations have taken variations of the name *National Baptist:* the National Baptist Convention of the United States of America, Inc.; the National Baptist Convention of America; the National Missionary Baptist Convention; and the Progressive National Baptist Convention, Inc.

The National Baptist Convention of the United States of America, Inc. (NBCUSA) is the largest African American denomination in America. The National Baptist Convention was established in Atlanta, Georgia, on September 28, 1895. This event marked the successful merger of three separate Baptist organizations: the Foreign Mission Baptist Convention of 1880, the American National Baptist Convention of 1886 and the Baptist National Educational Convention of 1893. In 2003 it numbered an estimated 7,000,000 members in over 30,000 congregations.

In 1915 the Convention divided into two separate organizations following a dispute over the ownership of the National Baptist Publishing Board. Under the leadership of Reverend R. H. Boyd, corresponding secretary of the Convention's publication board and a skillful businessman, the publishing house had become a highly successful business, raising over $2 million within the first ten years of its existence. Tensions emerged between Boyd and the Convention when the publishing house failed to donate its substantial funds to other denominational projects, or comply with the charter of the Convention. Attempting to establish its legal right to the publishing house, the Convention adopted a new charter, redefined the charge of the publishing board and incorporated itself as the National Baptist Convention of the United States of America, Incorporated. Boyd and his constituents rejected the new charter, withdrew the publishing house from the newly incorporated Convention and designated themselves the National Baptist Convention of America, Unincorporated (now "Incorporated") (NBCA). In 2003, the NBCA claimed over 2.5 million members and over 11,000 congregations (although another study claimed that the NBCA was much smaller).

These two denominational organizations, the NBCUSA and the NBCA, continue to function as distinctive bodies into the twenty-first century, though they share basic Baptist theological beliefs such as the authority of the Bible, the lordship of Jesus Christ, the baptism of believers, the separation of church and state, and the autonomy of local church and state associations.

The Progressive National Baptist Convention Incorporated (PNBC) emerged in 1961, following a five-year debate within the NBCUSA over policies regarding the election of officers and the length of the Convention president's term in office. In 1957 Dr. J. H. Jackson, who had already served a four-year term as the NBCUSA president, ruled against the 1952 policy restricting a president's term in office to four years. Many in the NBCUSA, among them Dr. G. C. Taylor, felt that this was a return to practices that predated the 1952 policy when presidents served for life. This discontent led to heated debates at the 1960 convention in Kansas City, Missouri, and an invitation from a convention member, Dr. L. Venchael Booth of Zion Baptist Church in Cincinnati, Ohio, for all dissatisfied delegates to attend a meeting at his church. Thirty-three delegates from fourteen states attended that meeting and formed the PNBC.

Though there is little doctrinal disagreement between the PNBC and its parent body, the two organizations do show dissimilarities at the level of organization. The PNBC elects its officers every two years and limits the Convention president's term in office to eight years. In 2003 the PNBC was composed of more than 1,800 churches and a membership of over 2,500,000.

In 1988 the NBCUSA and the NBCA were discussing the possibility of a union when a dispute occurred in the National Baptist Convention of America over the control of the National Baptist Publishing Board. When a group of prominent pastors and many of the presidents of various NBCA boards and auxiliaries walked out, all talk of union was indefinitely postponed. The dispute resulted in the formation of the National Missionary Baptist Convention of America (NMBCA), whose first convention was held in 1989. The NMBCA reports an estimated 260 churches with 80,000 members.

NBCUSA
White Rock Baptist Church Office
5240 Chestnut Street
Philadelphia, PA 19139
Phone: (215) 474-5785
Fax: (215) 474-3332
Website: www.nationalbaptist.com

NBCA
1320 Pierre Ave.
Shreveport, LA 71103
Phone: (318) 221-3701
Fax: (318) 222-7512
Website: www.nbcamerica.org

PNBC
601 50th St. NE
Washington, DC 20019
Phone: (800) 876-7622
Website: www.pnbc.org

NMBCA
4269 South Figueroa St.
Los Angeles, CA 90037
Phone: (888) 760-0007
Fax: (323) 235-8907
Website: www.nbca.com

National Missionary Baptist Church of America. *See* National Baptists.

National Primitive Baptists. See Primitive Baptists.

O

Old Mennonite Church. *See* Mennonite Church.

Orthodox Church in America. The Patriarchate of Moscow granted autocephaly (the status of a self-governing local Orthodox church having the right to elect its own primate) to the jurisdiction in America known as the Metropolia on April 10, 1970. Since then it has used the title The Orthodox Church in America (OAC). It is the second-largest Orthodox jurisdiction in America.

The Metropolia, known formally as the Russian Orthodox Greek Catholic Church, claimed to be the direct continuation of the Alaskan Mission established by the Church of Russia in 1794. The Metropolia broke relations with the Church of Russia in 1924 and was viewed as being schismatic by the latter from the year 1933. Between 1937 and 1946 the Metropolia became associated with the Russian Orthodox Church Outside of Russia. By the year 1970 the Metropolia was one of at least twelve Orthodox jurisdictions in America, each of which had a direct or indirect link to an autocephalous mother church in Europe. Viewing the Metropolia as its daughter jurisdiction, the Church of Russia claimed to have the right to grant it an autocephalous status in 1970.

The autocephaly of the Metropolia was subsequently recognized by the autocephalous Churches of Bulgaria, Georgia and Poland. However, the autocephaly has not been recognized by the autocephalous Churches of Constantinople, Alexandria, Antioch, Jerusalem,

Serbia, Romania, Cyprus and Greece. These latter churches have not broken communion with the Metropolia but simply refuse to recognize its autocephalous status.

The OCA comprises fifteen diocese, and in the past two decades it has established over 220 new parishes, claiming a total of approximately 700 parishes, communities and other institutions in North America.

P.O. Box 675
Syosset, NY 11791-0675
Phone: (516) 922-0550; Fax: (516) 922-0954
Website: www.oca.org

Orthodox Presbyterian Church. A small Presbyterian denomination with roots in the fundamentalist-modernist controversy. The Orthodox Presbyterian Church (OPC) was founded on June 11, 1936, in the aftermath of a 1929 controversy in which a group of professors at Princeton Theological Seminary, led by J. Gresham Machen, left that seminary to establish Westminster Theological Seminary

Paramount among the reasons for that action was the conviction of Machen and his colleagues that Princeton and the Presbyterian Church (USA), of which Princeton was the leading seminary, had departed from historic Christianity. The particular matters at issue were their adoption of a weak view of the authority of Scripture and rejection of significant doctrines such as the virgin birth of Christ. Originally calling itself the Presbyterian Church of America, the new body was forced by court action to discontinue use of that name in 1939, and it adopted in its place the name Orthodox Presbyterian Church.

The OPC has, since its inception, been best known for its vigorous affirmation of the truths of historic Christianity and Reformed orthodoxy as they are expressed in the Westminster Confession of Faith and catechisms. The denomination utilizes three standing committees representing the fundamental emphases within the OPC: world missions, home missions and Christian education. In 2002 the OPC had over 26,000 communicant members in approximately 237 congregations throughout the U.S.

607 N. Easton Rd., Bldg E, Box P
Willow Grove, PA 19090
Phone: (215) 830-0900 ; Fax: (215) 830-0350
Website: www.opc.org

P

Pentecostal Assemblies of Canada. The largest Pentecostal denomination in Canada. The roots of the Pentecostal Assemblies of Canada lie in the evangelical world of the nineteenth century, with particular strength in the evangelistic emphasis of revivalism and missions, often from a Wesleyan and Holiness perspective. To this was added a millennial eschatology whose pessimistic view of church and society in this age interpreted the feelings of many and produced dissatisfaction with the whole system of denominations.

Canadian Pentecostalism, along with its associates around the world, was a Christian renewal movement. It brought its pessimistic worldview into harness with its renewal optimism by positing a brief period before the second advent of Christ, in which the church would be restored to apostolic fullness. This meant the active presence among Christians of the gifts of the Holy Spirit as described in 1 Corinthians 12, particularly signified by the gift of tongues.

The movement sprang up in Canada from 1906, with R. E. McAlister going to the Azusa Street meetings in Los Angeles and returning with the Pentecostal message to the receptive Ottawa Valley, with its Holiness heritage. A. H. Argue, a prominent businessman, went to William H. Durham's church in Chicago and returned to Winnipeg with the Pentecostal emphasis making it the seedbed not only of the Social Gospel but also of much of Canadian Pentecostalism. Meanwhile, from about 1906 James and Ellen Hebden were building a Pentecostal base at their Toronto mission hall.

As the movement spread, some kind of organization became necessary. In 1919 the Pentecostal Assemblies of Canada (PAOC) was chartered. This dynamic renewal movement was fortunate in its first educational venture, for its principal was J. E. Purdie, a well-trained evangelical Anglican, who laid excellent theological foundations under much of the denomination. The Assemblies have become the fastest-growing form of Canadian Christianity, with the total number of members and active nonmembers in 2001 being 232,000. The Pentecostal Assemblies of Newfoundland maintains a separate legal existence, but the two denominations are usually considered as one. Together they number 257,000—over 70 percent of all Canadian Pentecostals—with some 325 congregations

responding to pluralistic Canada by worshiping in a language
other than English.

2450 Milltower Court
Mississauga, Ontario L5N 5Z6
Phone: (905) 542-7400; Fax: (905) 542-7313
Website: www.paoc.org

Plymouth Brethren. An independent, nondenominational, evangelical movement. Dissatisfied with the formalism, clericalism and
spiritual dryness of many British churches in the early nineteenth
century, Christians of various groups met for Communion, prayer
and Bible teaching on a simple "New Testament" pattern. With centers in Dublin and Plymouth (the latter association giving them the
name they themselves do not use), the Brethren, or Christian Brethren, as some prefer to be called, developed into a separate movement by the 1830s.

The Brethren were united in the practice of weekly Communion
and evangelical on central points of doctrine, but the movement split
in the 1840s over church discipline. Since then it has fragmented further, with two types dominating. One group ("Exclusive"), who welcome to Communion only members of their own churches, are assemblies in a Circle of Fellowship directed by leaders who make
decisions for the constituent churches. The other, larger group
("Open") welcome all professing Christians to Communion and are
autonomous assemblies who join in common projects (usually the
sponsoring of Bible conferences, camps or missions).

J. N. Darby, an Exclusive leader, developed dispensationalism,
the theology most popular throughout the movement. Open Brethren emphasize evangelism and missions and have been influential
in many evangelical organizations. Brethren do not observe a
clergy-laity distinction but have recognized some believers as gifted
and called to preach and often have supported them in full-time
itinerant Bible teaching or evangelism. Recently, some Open assemblies have called seminary trained men as resident pastoral workers. There are an estimated 1,150 congregations with 100,000 members in the U.S., and 600 congregations with 50,000 members in
Canada. The Plymouth Brethren support Emmaus Bible College in
Dubuque, Iowa.

Presbyterian Church in America. A Conservative Presbyterian denomination, organized December 1973 as the National Presbyterian Church. The present name dates from the second general assembly (1974). The denomination had its origin in the "continuing church" movement, a conservative effort in the Presbyterian Church in the U.S. (PCUS) (the "Southern Presbyterian" Church) opposed to the denomination's perceived departures from historic doctrines, its membership in the National and World Councils of Churches and to social and political pronouncements by church bodies.

The division that gave rise to the new denomination was encouraged mainly by four conservative organizations: *Presbyterian Journal,* Presbyterian Evangelistic Fellowship, Concerned Laymen and Presbyterian Churchmen United. As early as 1969 several hundred ministers and church sessions signed a "Declaration of Commitment," opposing union with the United Presbyterian Church in the U.S.A. (UPCUSA), membership in the Consultation on Christian Union and substantial change in the doctrinal standards of the PCUS. Several rallies and caucuses were held in the interest of the movement, and the leadership recommended that churches withdraw during 1973 (while the PCUS was engaged in union talks with the UPCUSA and was drafting a possible new confession of faith) by renouncing their membership in the PCUS. Many churches, however, requested and received dismissal.

After plans were laid at a convocation of sessions in Atlanta in May 1973, an advisory convention met in Asheville, North Carolina, in August 1973, and the first general assembly met in Birmingham, Alabama, in December 1973. The first assembly adopted a "Message to All Churches of Jesus Christ throughout the World" that took issue with the PCUS regarding "a diluted theology, a gospel tending towards humanism, an unbiblical view of marriage and divorce, the ordination of women, financing of abortion . . . and numerous other non-Biblical positions . . . all traceable to a different view of Scripture from that we hold and that which was held by the Southern Presbyterian forefathers." The assembly enunciated its stand for the inerrancy of the Bible, the Reformed faith of the Westminster Standards, the spirituality of the church, the historical Presbyterian view of church government and "the practice of the principle of purity in the Church visible."

Some independent churches and presbyteries, as well as congregations from other denominations, have joined the denomination. The denomination was augmented in 1982 by reception of the Reformed Presbyterian Church, Evangelical Synod (itself the result of a 1965 merger between the Reformed Presbyterian Church, General Synod and the former Evangelical Presbyterian Church, not to be confused with the present-day *Evangelical Presbyterian Church). The union also brought Covenant College (Lookout Mountain, Tennessee) and Covenant Seminary (St. Louis, Missouri) into the denomination. Efforts thus far to bring the *Orthodox Presbyterian Church into the denomination have been unsuccessful.

The Presbyterian Church in America (PCA) is now a national church, the second-largest Presbyterian denomination in the U.S. In 1973 there were about 260 churches, 41,000 members and 196 ministers. In 2001 there were 1,498 churches, 306,784 members and 3,082 ministers. The PCA is strongly committed to missions, to the equality in position and authority of ministers and ruling elders, and to the rights of local congregations. The offices of the church are in Decatur, Georgia.

1700 N. Brown Rd., Suite 105
Lawrenceville, GA 30043-8122
Phone: (678) 825-1000
Website: www.pcanet.org

Presbyterian Church in Canada. Canada's major Presbyterian denomination. Canadian Presbyterianism arose first in Nova Scotia in the mid-eighteenth century. It followed the patterns of migration from the U.S. and the United Kingdom, but the predominant numbers and influence came from the Church of Scotland. Indeed, much of Canadian Presbyterian history mirrors that of the Scottish church. In 1875 the major Presbyterian bodies in Canada united to form the Presbyterian Church in Canada, a denomination independent of, if still in contact with, the Scottish church.

Fifty years later, the formation of the *United Church of Canada split the Presbyterian church into two groups: the larger one went into union with the major Methodist and Congregational bodies, while about a third remained as "continuing" Presbyterians.

A number of theological traditions have found a home in Canadian Presbyterianism. Liberal theology, emerging in Presbyterian seminaries around the turn of the twentieth century, remained in those seminaries and increased its influence on continuing Presbyterianism after the birth of the United Church. Traditional Presbyterian orthodoxy as well as evangelicalism have characterized other parts of the church. Evangelicalism in particular has been manifest in the recently organized Renewal Fellowship. And Canadian Presbyterianism saw the rise of an indigenous form of neo-orthodox theology, preeminently in the work of W. W. Bryden, former professor and principal of Knox College, Toronto. While some twentieth-century evangelicals and others have reacted against what they saw as an overemphasis on social ministry, the church has always sought to wrestle with the social problems of the day, whether Prohibition, poor relief, preservation of the Lord's Day Act or the emancipation of women.

Once the largest Protestant denomination in Canada, the Presbyterian Church has lost members steadily since the early 1960s. In the early 2000s it claimed over 960 churches and an inclusive membership of over 198,000. It is a member of the World Alliance of Reformed Churches and of the Canadian and World Councils of Churches.

50 Wynford Dr.
Toronto, Ontario M3C 1J7
Phone: (800) 619-7301 or (416) 441-1111
Fax: (416) 441-2825
Website: www.presbyterian.ca

Presbyterian Church (U.S.A.). A mainline Presbyterian denomination formed from 1983 to 1987 by the union of the United Presbyterian Church in the United States of America (UPCUSA) and the Presbyterian Church in the United States (PCUS), also known as the "Southern Presbyterian Church."

The present-day Presbyterian Church (U.S.A.) (PCUSA) traces its roots back to 1788 and the formation of the Presbyterian General Assembly, and further yet to the Presbytery, gathered in 1706. Representing the connectional side of Puritanism and the Scottish Presbyterian traditions, the Presbytery constituted itself a synod in 1716 and grew during colonial times to become a significant force in American religion. Throughout the varied fortunes of the Presbyterian Church, the General Assembly has remained the major judicatory body among Presbyterian bodies from 1788 until the present day.

The Second Great Awakening proved costly for the Presbyterians, whose leadership opposed the emotional demonstrations of conversion and the lack of attention to theology. Many members left to join the Restoration Movement, which led to the forming of the *Disciples of Christ and other "Campbellite" bodies. Other Presbyterians became Baptists, Methodists and even Shakers. In 1803-1810 some Presbyterians withdrew to form the *Cumberland Presbyterian Church, a separate body whose General Assembly voted in 1906 to rejoin what had by then come to be called the Presbyterian Church in the U.S.A. (PC-USA) (about two-thirds of them did rejoin). In the 1830s disputes in the PC-USA about theology, relations with other Christian bodies and reform methods regarding slavery led to another split—into Old School and New School assemblies. Generally more parochial in missionary programs, Old School Presbyterians also proved less willing to work against slavery and more closely tied to the *Westminster Confession of Faith.*

Most Presbyterians in the South belonged to Old School assemblies. After the taking of Fort Sumpter and the secession of several states to form the Confederacy in 1861, the Old School in the South became the Presbyterian Church in the Confederate States of America, later taking the name Presbyterian Church in the U.S. (PCUS) in 1866. After the Civil War, Old and New School assemblies in the North reunited into one denomination, the PC-USA (1870), and their mission work in the South among African Americans soon led to the PC-USA again being a truly national religious body. In 1910, after the reunion with most of the Cumberland Presbyterians, the PC-USA numbered 1.4 million.

The United Presbyterian Church in the United States of America (UPCUSA), emerged from the union of the PC-USA and the United Presbyterian Church of North America (UPCNA) in 1958. The UPCNA had been formed in 1858 by Scottish Covenanter Presbyterians who had come to terms with their American environment and joined together.

The PC-USA, more than other Reformed denominations, was the

scene of struggles between fundamentalists and so-called modernists. In 1936 a group of conservative Presbyterians, led by J. Gresham Machen, withdrew to form what is known today as the *Orthodox Presbyterian Church. A group withdrew from that body in 1937 to form the Bible Presbyterian Church. The PCUS suffered the withdrawal of a number of conservative members and congregations in the 1970s. Objecting to a number of changes in the church's policies and doctrinal emphases, as well as attempts to join with the more liberal UPCUSA, they left to join the newly formed *Presbyterian Church in America.

Their departure enabled the PCUS, which had previously rejected union with the Northern Presbyterians in the 1950s, to join with the UPCUSA to form the Presbyterian Church (U.S.A.) on June 10, 1983. The gradual process of consolidating national offices, boards and agencies, as well as merging overlapping synods and presbyteries, continued into the late 1980s. In 2002 the PCUSA reported 11,097 congregations with an inclusive membership of 2,451,969.

100 Witherspoon Street
Louisville, KY 40202-1396
Phone: (800) 872-3283
Website: www.pcusa.org

Primitive Baptists. Baptist churches and associations generally characterized by rigid predestinarianism and a desire to recapture the original faith and order of the New Testament apostles. Emerging in the early nineteenth century, these Baptists used Particular Baptist confessions to develop a rigid Calvinism and an opposition to organized missions. The Kehuckee Association (North Carolina), which first articulated their position (1826), said missionary organizations promoted a nonpredestinarian theology, undermined local church autonomy and encouraged a paid clergy. Most Primitive Baptists oppose church auxiliaries not found in Scripture, such as Bible and tract societies, seminaries, and Sunday schools. Their churches group only in associations that meet annually and correspond with each other by letter or messenger. Their church order has been characterized by simple, monthly worship meetings, closed communion, refusal to accept members without Primitive Baptist immersion, and untrained and unsalaried, bivocational ministers.

Today four Primitive Baptist groups total about 50,000 members: a few descendants of Daniel Parker's "Two-Seed-in-the-Spirit Predestinarian Baptists" (c. 1826) still exist in Texas and Louisiana; the rigidly predestinarian Absoluters number a few thousand; the Old Liners, who allow human responsibility in predestination, make up the great majority; and the second-largest group, Progressive Primitive Baptists, are the least rigidly predestinarian, meet weekly, pay ministerial salaries and conduct Sunday schools. A fifth group, the National Primitive Baptists, an African American convention, dwarfs the others with over one million members. Its headquarters are located in Huntsville, Alabama.

P.O. Box 38
Thornton, AR 71766
Phone: (501) 352-3694
Website: www.primitivebaptist.org

Progressive National Baptist Convention, Incorporated. *See* National Baptists.

Protestant Episcopal Church in the U.S.A. Alternately called the Episcopal Church, the Protestant Episcopal Church in the U.S.A. is a member of the worldwide fellowship of Anglican Churches. It is not joined to other Anglican churches through any established and regulated hierarchical organization. Rather, it is united to the Anglican Communion by a kinship of faith, government and worship through mutual association with the mother church in England.

The Episcopal Church began in America as an extension of the Church of England and under its jurisdiction. The first permanently organized Anglican church began in Jamestown, Virginia (1607). Other churches were established in Boston (1689), Philadelphia (1695), New York City (1697) and Newport (1702). By the end of the colonial period, Anglican churches were to be found in all thirteen colonies.

During the American Revolution, the church went through a severe crisis. Most clergy in the North, as opposed to their mostly patriotic brethren in the South, remained loyal to the King of England and closed their churches rather than remove prayers for the monarch from the liturgy. For this loyalty some were put in prison, some were banished from the colonies, and others escaped to Canada. However, a good many Episcopal lay people supported the Revolution and two-thirds of the signers of the Declaration of Independence were Episcopalians. In the end those colonies where Anglicanism had become the legally established religion (Virginia, Maryland, Georgia, North Carolina, South Carolina and certain counties of New York) were forced to revoke this status of the church.

After the Revolution the church gathered its forces to create a denomination independent and autonomous of the Church of England. The first general convention met in Philadelphia on September 27, 1785, and took preliminary steps toward the establishment of a duly recognized denomination. From the start the process took on a distinctly American character. When the general convention met it was attended by laity as well as clergy—a democratic arrangement without precedent in England. By the time of the next general convention in Philadelphia (1789), two bishops had been consecrated in England, a constitution was adopted, canons of the church were ratified, and a revised version of the Book of Common Prayer was authorized.

In organization the church is episcopal, meaning it is governed by bishops. Each bishop oversees a diocese (there are no archbishops or archdiocese) consisting of clergy and parishes. A general convention of bishops and laypeople, meeting every three years, presides over the whole church. This body consists of two houses, the House of Bishops (consisting of the bishops of each diocese) and the House of Deputies (consisting of four priests and four lay persons from every diocese). All actions of the church must be passed by both houses. A national council headed by the elected presiding bishop of the House of Bishops carries out the day-by-day administration of the church.

During the nineteenth century the Episcopal Church expanded with the growth and development of the U.S. missionary work, carried out by missionary bishops and priests, extended into the Midwest, the South and the Southwest. Between 1829 and 1860 the number of Episcopalians increased from 30,000 to nearly 150,000. Schools were also founded, with General Theological Seminary of New York

(1819) representing the high church movement and the Theological Seminary of Virginia (1824) nourishing the evangelical movement. While the Civil War separated Episcopalians into northern and southern factions, they quietly resumed full relations when the war ended. By 1900 the church had grown to 720,000 communicants.

In the twentieth century the church has been deeply involved in the ecumenical movement. Its platform for unity calls for the union of the church around four basic principles: (1) the Scriptures as the Word of God, (2) the primitive creeds as the rule of faith, (3) the two sacraments ordained by Christ, and (4) the episcopate. The Episcopal Church is a member of the World Council of Churches, the National Council of Churches and Churches Uniting in Christ.

Doctrinally the Episcopal Church holds to the ancient creeds, particularly the Apostles' and Nicene Creeds, as appropriate historic symbols of faith. The Thirty-nine Articles of the Reformation are loosely held, but are not at all binding on the clergy. A wide variety of interpretation is tolerated in the Episcopal Church, a fact represented by the presence of evangelicals, charismatics, liberals and Anglo-Catholics in the church. What binds the church together and defines its unity is its worship, as articulated in the Book of Common Prayer (revised 1979).

In 2000 the Episcopal Church had an inclusive membership of 2,333,327 (with 1,877,271 full communicants) in 7,364 churches.

815 Second Ave.
New York, NY 10017
Phone: (800) 334-7626; Fax: (212) 867-0395
Website: www.ecusa.anglican.org

Q

Quakers. *See* Evangelical Friends International; Friends General Conference; Religious Society of Friends.

R

Reformed Church in America. The Reformed Church in America (RCA) has its origin in the formation of a Dutch Reformed congregation on Manhattan Island by Jonas Michaelius in 1628. Michaelius was followed in time by other pastors as the Dutch settlers moved west into New Jersey, north along the Hudson River to Albany and east into Long Island. Although Dutch settlers virtually ceased coming to America after the Netherlands lost control of New Netherland to the English in 1664, a good number of congregations took root in New York and New Jersey.

With the coming of the English, Americanization was inevitable for the Dutch churches as well as for the French and German Reformed congregations that joined the denomination in the later seventeenth and early eighteenth centuries. But the process led to conflict. The churches and pastors were divided between the *conferentie*, who wished to maintain Dutch ways and remain within the classis of Amsterdam, and the *coetus* churches, who wished to organize an American body (called a "classis") and educate ministerial recruits in America rather than sending them back to the Netherlands to be educated by the mother church. The warring groups were brought together in the Union Convention of 1772.

The American Revolution and the independence of the thirteen colonies eventually led to the independence of the Dutch Church and their organization into a distinct body in 1792. Queens College was chartered in New Brunswick, New Jersey, in 1766. A theological seminary was established in Brooklyn in (1784). In 1856 the seminary at New Brunswick separated from Queens College, which had changed its name to Rutgers College in 1825.

Although a number of Dutch Reformed people moved to the West and formed congregations in Illinois, Kentucky, Michigan and Wisconsin, many Reformed Christians readily joined the Congregational and Presbyterian churches because Dutch Reformed congregations were few and far between in the West. Had it not been for the new Dutch migration in the mid-nineteenth century, which added many members and new congregations, the old Dutch Reformed Church might have merged with another Reformed denomination by the end of the century and lost its identity. In 1867 the Dutch Reformed Church dropped the word *Dutch* from its title and began to call itself the Reformed Church in America.

Beginning in 1847 a new surge of Dutch and German Reformed

immigrants moved into the Midwest and settled in Western Michigan and Pella, Iowa. Most of these new settlers had been members of the "Afscheiding," or separatist movement, which seceded from the state church of the Netherlands in 1834. Strongly orthodox and pious, the newcomers immediately formed congregations.

These separatists were encouraged to unite with the old Dutch Church in the East. The classis of Holland (Michigan) was accepted into the Dutch Reformed Church in 1850. In time, the western churches were successful in establishing Western Theological Seminary and Hope College in Holland, Michigan; Central College in Pella, Iowa; and Northwestern College in Orange City, Iowa.

However, in 1857 some members showed their dislike of the Union of 1850 by seceding and forming the *Christian Reformed Church. In 1882 a dispute over the issue of allowing Masons to be members of the Reformed Church resulted in a sizable group leaving the denomination to join the Christian Reformed Church.

Since its formal organization in 1792, the RCA has adhered to the Heidelberg Catechism, the Belgic Confession and the Canons of the Synod of Dort. Although the denomination holds a conservative, orthodox, Reformed stance, the continual Americanization of the church shows the effects of other theological trends. But in spite of the strength of several theological trends contrary to Reformed orthodoxy, only contemporary evangelicalism has made any major impact on the RCA. Perhaps surprisingly, the contemporary positive thinking movement has been most visibly represented by two prominent RCA ministers, Norman Vincent Peale and Robert H. Schuller.

The RCA was a charter member of the Federal Council of Churches (1908), the World Council of Churches (1948) and the National Council of Churches (1950). The denomination currently enrolls about 290,000 communicant and baptized members in approximately 900 churches.

New York City: (800) 722-9977
Fax: (212) 870-2499
Website: www.rca.org

Reformed Episcopal Church. An evangelical Episcopal Church organized in 1873. In reaction to the influence of the Tractarian Movement in the Protestant Episcopal Church in the U.S.A., evangelical Episcopalians organized a series of protests between 1843 and 1873. Evangelicals clashed with those of Tractarian sympathies over ritual, doctrine and vestments, while calling for a wider Protestant ecumenicity and greater liberty in the use and meaning of critical passages of the Book of Common Prayer.

These clashes culminated in October 1873 with the public censure of Bishop George David Cummins of Kentucky by Bishop H. Potter of New York for participating in an ecumenical Communion service connected with the Evangelical Alliance. Cummins resigned his office on November 10, 1873, to transfer his episcopate to "another sphere," and organized the Reformed Episcopal Church (REC) with six other clergymen and twenty laymen on December 2, 1873, for the "purpose of restoring the old paths of their fathers."

A *Declaration of Principles* (condemning transubstantiation in the Eucharist, moral regeneration in baptism and the exclusive validity of episcopal government) was issued by Cummins and remains the founding document of the church. A Constitution and Canons and a slightly amended Book of Common Prayer were adopted in 1874. By 1876 the REC comprised seven jurisdictions in the U.S. and Canada. It currently has approximately 6,400 members in three synods and a national missionary jurisdiction, and is in communion with several other evangelical Anglican bodies abroad. The orders of the Reformed Episcopal Church have generally been acknowledged as valid by the Episcopal Church.

211 Byrne Ave.
Houston, TX 77009
Phone: (800) 732-3433; Fax: (713) 862-4929
Website: www.recus.org

Reformed Presbyterian Church in North America. A Reformed denomination with roots in Scottish Presbyterianism. Deriving mainly from dissenting Scottish Covenanters coming to America in the 1700s, the first congregation was organized in Lancaster County, Pennsylvania, in 1743. The Reformed Presbytery, established in 1774, was characterized by exclusive psalm singing, genuine piety and nonparticipation in any civil government that refused to acknowledge the "crown rights" of Christ.

Soon after the 1809 formation of the Synod of the Reformed Presbyterian Church, some leaders began viewing nonparticipation in government (e.g., voting and jury duty) as a hindrance to evangelism. A division ensued in 1833, in which part of the denomination embraced the government-participation view and were called "new lights." This group adopted the name Reformed Presbyterian Church in North America, General Synod (RPC, GS). The Reformed Presbyterian Church of North America (RPCNA) remained true to its Covenanter roots of nonparticipation in any organization that did not recognize the Lordship of Jesus Christ. Another major split occurred in 1892 when a sizable group joined the United Presbyterian Church.

In 1800 the RPCNA took a strong stand against slavery, and many members supported the Underground Railroad. The RPCNA holds to the inerrancy of Scripture and looks to the Westminster Confession of Faith for doctrinal guidance. It publishes a Testimony that explains its Reformed distinctives. In worship, the church is noninstrumental and sings only from Psalms. The church sponsors Geneva College in Beaver Falls, Pennsylvania, Reformed Theological Seminary in Pittsburgh, Pennsylvania, and Ottawa Theological Hall in Ottawa, Canada. As of 1997 there were 86 churches with an inclusive membership of 6,105.

7408 Penn Avenue
Pittsburgh, PA 15208
Phone: (412) 731-1177; Fax: (412) 731-8861
Website: www.rpcna.org

Regular Baptists. Calvinistic Baptists opposed to the emotionalism and evangelistic invitations of the Great Awakening. In contrast to revivalistic Separate Baptists, Regular Baptists were more urbane and more orderly in worship, supported educated and salaried ministers, and discouraged women from ministering publicly. Initially strongest in the Middle Colonies, they were influenced by the Philadelphia Association (1707), from which itinerant preachers planted churches in Virginia (1740s), North Carolina (1750s), Georgia (1770s) and on the Kentucky-Tennessee frontier (1780s). Also influential were Charleston (1751), Warren (1767), and Kehuckee (1769) associations. By 1800 most Regulars and Separates had merged on the basis of the Philadelphia Confession (1742).

Today Regular Baptists comprise a cultural-religious movement that preserves rural folkways through monthly worship, plaintive singing, sing-song preaching, community gatherings and annual association fellowship. They include Old Regular Baptists, mainly of Appalachia (1980: 19,770 members, 366 churches); United Baptists, found from Kentucky through Missouri (1993: 63,641 members, 586 churches); and the General Association of (Duck River) Baptists in Alabama, Tennessee, Georgia and Mississippi (1993: 10,508 members, 100 churches).

General Association of Regular Baptist Churches
1300 North Meacham Road
Schaumburg, IL 60173-4806
Phone: (888) 588-1600 or (847) 843-1600
Website: www.garbc.org

Religious Society of Friends. The Society of Friends was one of many religious groups that arose from the ferment of the English Puritan revolution. The movement dates its origin from 1652 when George Fox, standing atop Pendle Hill, received a vision of "a great people to be gathered" in Northwest England. The nickname "Quaker," originally used in 1647 of a sect of women in England who reportedly shivered and shook in religious excitement, was first used in 1650 to describe the Friends because they too were known to tremble when they fell under the power of God. "Friends" or "Society of Friends" is the preferred title.

Fox thirsted after the divine life but was tormented by temptation and despair. He undertook a troubled quest for infallible religious authority and met the most renowned religious teachers of his day. But when he had despaired of all human help, he heard a voice which said, "There is one, even Christ Jesus, who can speak to thy condition." Through this experience Fox came to trust the immediate spiritual presence of Jesus Christ above every outward form and human teacher.

The burden of Fox's preaching was to turn every person to the Light of Christ within. The Light was not natural in the sense of being an inherent part of man, such as conscience, nor was it merely the spiritual side of human nature. The Light was the transcendent God perceptibly breaking into human consciousness.

Fox taught that both Spirit and Scripture spoke with one voice, but that the Scripture could only be properly understood and applied by one who stood in right spiritual relationship with God. He tirelessly stressed that the Scriptures are not the Word of God but rather point to Jesus Christ.

Fox taught that only obedience to Christ could make one a true Christian. Biblical proficiency was insufficient. True worship meant quiet waiting on the Spirit of God and could not be produced by human will. True worship was to apply oneself in silence directly to Jesus Christ to receive his grace and know his will. Fox believed that the Spirit always speaks in harmony with Christ's teachings as recorded in Scripture.

Almost immediately after the movement was born, Quakers began immigrating to America. Persecuted by Boston Puritans, by 1657 a number of Quakers found a tolerant home in Rhode Island. Within a few years they had won many converts in southern Massachusetts.

When William Penn, the most prominent Quaker in American history, received a charter for his colony of Pennsylvania in 1681, it immediately became a haven for persecuted Quakers and other religious groups. The colony thrived under religious tolerance and set a persuasive example for the developing nation. Indeed, many features of Pennsylvania's government were incorporated into the Constitution and Bill of Rights.

Many nineteenth-century Quakers provided leadership for the abolitionist movement, including the poet John Greenleaf Whittier, Levi Coffin, president of the Underground Railroad, and the early feminists Angelina and Sarah Grimké.

Quakers, believing that the gift of ministry is not distributed according to gender, have fostered female leadership since the movement's earliest days. Fox's first convert was a woman, and Quakers have had women preachers ever since. Quaker women, accustomed to equality and independent thought, provided a disproportionate number of women's rights leaders, including Lucretia Mott, Abby Kelly, Susan B. Anthony and Alice Paul.

Though presently numbering slightly more than 100,000 members in the U.S., there is as much theological diversity among American Quakers as there is among Protestants generally. The *Evangelical Friends International includes 36,000 members. *Friends General Conference is the liberal wing and includes 32,000 members. Worship in these meetings is generally silent and without reliance on paid leadership or prepared messages. Friends United Meeting, which roughly corresponds theologically to mainline Protestantism, includes 40,000 American members. Some Yearly Meetings hold dual membership in Friends United Meeting and Friends General Conference. The number of members of Yearly Meetings with joint membership is 17,400. Another 6,700 American Quakers belong to congregations that are unaffiliated with any of these major bodies. The Conservative Friends are the smallest group, comprising 1,500 members. They share many of the attitudes and attributes of Old Order Mennonites and Old German Baptists. Including all of these groups, there are about 1,000 Quaker congregations in the U.S.

Friends General Conference
1216 Arch St. #2B
Philadelphia, PA 19107
Website: www.fgcquaker.org

Friends United Meeting
101 Quaker Hill Dr.
Richmond, IN 47374
Website: www.fum.org

Roman Catholic Church. Roman Catholicism arrived in what is now the U.S. with sixteenth- and seventeenth-century Spanish and French explorers. The first permanent settlement in the continental U.S. was at St. Augustine, Florida, in 1565.

In 1776 American Catholics numbered about 25,000, one percent of the population of English America. There were twenty-three priests. The nation expanded rapidly, and more Catholics were added by the Louisiana Purchase (1803), annexation of Texas (1845), agreement with Britain on the Oregon Territory (1848) and the Mexican cession (1848).

Between 1820 and 1920, ten million Catholics arrived from Europe. Irish and Germans came first. In terms of numbers, the Roman Catholic Church was the largest in the country by 1850. Priests, as well as vowed religious sisters and brothers, accompanied all the immigrant groups, and they were instrumental in fashioning a more pluralistic mosaic of American Catholicism. Post-World War II Catholics shared in the socioeconomic upswing, the move to the suburbs and the religious revival of the 1950s. And with the election

(1960) of Roman Catholic John F. Kennedy as president, the Americanization was essentially complete.

The Second Vatican Council (1962-1965), called by Pope John XXIII, was a catalyst for extensive change. As American Catholics moved to suburbs, the role of the parish as social center declined. Parochial school costs rose. A downward trend in vocations to religious communities, the broader range of ministries (but not priesthood) open to women and increased lay participation altered institutional appearances, while virtual abandonment of Latin and greater informality in worship changed age-old patterns.

A sharper ideological spectrum has emerged. On the far right, small schisms emerged of those discontented with worship reforms and what they see as a leftward political drift in the Church. Prolife activists count many Catholics among them. While most American Catholics are religiously centrist, there is greater liberalism in ethical areas and in judging what is, or is not, sinful—and more reliance on individual conscience instead of unquestioning obedience to church directives. Both social-activist liberals and right-wing intellectuals actively propagate their ideas in journals and in Washington, D.C., think tanks. There is growing interest in personal spirituality, nourished by groups that promote Bible study, charismatic prayer and family and parish renewal. Houses of prayer and spiritual retreat centers flourish.

In 2003 American Catholics numbered about 66.4 million in 19,484 parishes with 44,500 priests. Each parish belongs to a diocese that is headed by a bishop. The bishop is the head of the diocese, overseeing the priests and the faithful within the diocese. Bishops are appointed by the bishop of Rome, the pope, who is the head of the Roman Catholic Church. American bishops are part of the United States Catholic Conference of Bishops, headquartered in Washington, D.C.

Roman Catholics are orthodox Christians guided by Scripture and tradition. However, they differ from Protestants in several ways; among these are (1) the identifcation of the bishop of Rome as the head of the universal church, (2) seven sacraments—baptism, confirmation, communion, penance, marriage, holy orders (for those being ordained to ministry), and anointing of the sick (for the seriously ill), (3) the transubstantiation of the bread and wine of communion into the actual body and blood of Christ, (4) the veneration of and prayer to Mary (and the saints), and (5) a celibate priesthood.

U.S. Catholic Conference of Bishops
3211 4th St., NE
Washington, DC 20017-1194
Phone: (202) 541-3000
Website: www.usccb.org

S

Salvation Army. Holiness denomination. The mission that became the Salvation Army was established in the slums of London, England, in 1865 by William Booth, an independent evangelist trained in Wesleyan doctrine, and his wife Catherine. The mission was given its present military form in 1878. The Army's official missionaries "opened fire" on the U.S. in March 1880, and on Canada in July 1882.

The Salvation Army may be described as a Protestant and evangelical denomination. Its members, both clergy ("Officers") and lay persons ("Soldiers"), are called "Salvationists." They subscribe to eleven specific doctrines, with an emphasis on the Wesleyan doctrine of sanctification. (They do not observe the Lord's Supper or baptism.) The purpose of the Salvation Army from the start has been to make converts for Christ from among those elements in society not touched by other forms of religion.

Practical charitable activities formed an important part of the Army's ministry from its earliest days. In recent years social relief work has come to occupy a large part of the time and energy of Army personnel and to figure prominently in the organization's public relations campaigns. One practical consequence of this emphasis has been, however—especially in the U.S.—that the Salvation Army is regarded by most of the general public as a charitable, rather than as a religious, organization.

The American Salvation Army had 5,000 active officers in 1998 with an inclusive membership of approximately 450,000. There are 1,200 "Corps"(local churches, which in the U.S. almost always form part of a larger community-center complex) in the United States.

The Salvation Army's social welfare services are especially well developed in the U.S. These include personal counseling, family welfare, day care, summer camps, senior citizens' residences, Christmas relief, assistance in times of natural disaster and an extensive residential program for homeless alcoholics.

615 Slaters Lane, P.O. Box 269
Alexandria, VA 22313
Phone: (703) 684-5500; Fax: (703) 684-5538
Website: www.salvationarmyusa.org

Schwenkfelders (The Schwenkfelder Church). Followers of the sixteenth-century spiritualist reformer Caspar Schwenckfeld von Ossig (1489-1561). Schwenckfeld was a well-educated and devout Silesian nobleman who was an independent thinker with strong mystical leanings and concerns about the fruits of Christian living. He eventually broke with his friend Luther and other Reformers, primarily over Christology and the nature of the Lord's Supper.

Like the Anabaptists, Schwenckfeld rejected infant baptism, participation in war and swearing of oaths; he advocated a strict separation of church and state. Unlike other radical reformers, however, Schwenkfeld's mysticism also led him to reject all forms of the "visible church," including believer's baptism. He taught that the sacraments are to be inwardly and spiritually observed only, a position not unlike the English *Quakers.

Though Schwenckfeld did not wish to organize a church, small, informal conventicles developed in Silesia, Swabia and Prussia. Persecution ended the movement in Europe, but a remnant group sought toleration in colonial Pennsylvania (1734). The Society of Schwenkfelders was formed in 1782 (incorporated 1909). In 1998 there were five congregations with approximately 3,000 members, all in southeastern Pennsylvania.

Schwenkfelder Library & Heritage Center
105 Seminary St.
Pennsburg, PA 18073
Phone: (215) 679-3103
Website: www.schwenfelder.com

Separate Baptists. Baptists originating among the prorevivalists of the Great Awakening. During the Great Awakening many Baptist churches split into revivalistic (Separate) and antirevivalistic (Regular) factions. The first identifiable Separate Baptist church resulted from such a schism (1743) in Boston. Many revivalistic New Light Congregationalists also became Separate Baptists. Highly evangelistic and moderately Calvinistic, Separate Baptists allowed women to preach, practiced "nine rites," and disdained a learned or paid ministry and confessionalism. Their emotional worship services typically ended with invitations for salvation.

Differences between *Regular and Separate Baptists were pronounced in the South, but barriers to fellowship eroded near the end of the eighteenth century. At that time most Separate Baptists moved toward a stronger Calvinism, adopted the Philadelphia Confession and entered Regular Baptist associations. Churches rejecting that union organized six associations in Tennessee, Kentucky, Indiana and Illinois. These formed the General Association of Separate Baptists (1912), which in 1975 added the Christian Unity Association (of North Carolina and Virginia). Generally conservative in theology, they practice foot washing. They maintain a mission board and a ministers' conference, but no central headquarters, colleges or seminaries. In 1992 they numbered 100 churches with about 8,000 members.

10102 N. Hickory Ln.
Columbus, IN 47203
Phone: (812) 526-2540
Website: www.separatebaptist.org

Seventh-day Adventists. Christian denomination originating in the U.S. that emphasizes Saturday as the sabbath and the imminent second coming of Christ. Seventh-day Adventism arose out of the nineteenth-century Millerite movement, which had predicted Christ's second coming about 1843-1844, the last significant date chosen being October 22, 1844. Through the work of James and Ellen White and Joseph Bates, a small group coalesced in the Northeast around several doctrines. By the early 1850s these distinctive beliefs included the seventh-day sabbath, the imminent personal advent of Christ, conditional immortality, the investigative judgment (referring to Christ's blotting out of sins, believed to have begun in 1844 in the heavenly sanctuary) and the spirit of prophecy as manifested in the work of

Ellen White. They also adopted such practices as baptism by immersion and the ordinances of footwashing and the Lord's Supper.

Despite opposition among the sabbatarian Adventists, James and Ellen White pushed for formal church organization. In 1860 the name Seventh-day Adventist was chosen, and by 1863 there were six state conferences, which in that year established a General Conference. The new denomination had 3,500 members.

Seventh-day Adventism spread throughout the U.S., but most quickly in the West, establishing schools and sanitariums (later hospitals) in many places. Its work among foreign-language groups in the U.S. led to expansion overseas. By 1900 there were missionaries on every continent, creating educational, publishing and medical institutions.

After 1900 a new administrative structure was established; local churches were grouped together into conferences, conferences into unions and the unions into the general conference, each organization based on representation from its constituent bodies. In the twentieth century, the primary growth of Seventh-day Adventism was outside the U.S., although Americans have continued to maintain primary influence within the church. In 2001, out of a worldwide membership of 4,598,935, the U.S. accounted for 900,985 members.

12501 Old Columbia Pike
Silver Spring, MD 20904-6600
Phone: (301) 680-6000
Website: www.adventist.org

Seventh Day Baptists. Baptists differing from mainstream Baptists primarily in their strict sabbath observance. The earliest American church emerged when Stephen Mumford and seven sabbatarians left Newport Baptist Church and called William Hiscox as pastor (1671). Initial centers of growth were Rhode Island, Philadelphia and New Jersey. After 1735 they briefly flourished in Ephrata, Pennsylvania. During the nineteenth century they opposed alcoholism, slavery and secret societies, and lost many members to *Seventh-day Adventists.

The General Conference of Seventh Day Baptists, organized in 1801, with headquarters in Janesville, Wisconsin, maintains societies for missions, publications and education, a Sabbath School

Board, a Women's Executive Board and a Center for Ministerial Education. They support two colleges in West Virginia and Wisconsin. Their "Statement of Belief" (1937) is theologically conservative.

Generally ecumenical, they became concerned about political activities of the National and World councils of churches and withdrew in 1973 and 1976 respectively. In 1993 the churches had 5,250 members in 90 churches in America.

3120 Kennedy Rd., P.O. Box 1678
Janesville, WI 53547-1678
Phone: (608) 752-5055; Fax: (608) 752-7711
Website: www.seventhdaybaptist.org

Shakers. Millenarian communal society. The Shakers (officially, The United Society of Believers in Christ's Second Appearing, or Millennial Church) originated in England as a loose union of enthusiasts under the leadership of *Quakers Jane and James Wardley. The group did not fare well until visionary member Ann Lee led a band of eight Shakers from Manchester, England, to New York in 1774, soon settling in the wilderness at Niskeyuna (near Albany). Over time they organized as a community, gained members through missionary efforts, grew and prospered.

Parallel lines of male and female authority characterized Shaker government from its early days. Equally notable was their understanding of God as Father-Mother, a truth they believed was best imaged in their dual-gender structure. But the Shakers are most remembered for their functional and gracefully simple furniture and handicrafts, and the lively Shaker worship, which included original hymns and dances.

The Shakers insisted that Christ had already come again, embodied in an embryonic way in the Shaker community. Some believed that Ann Lee was the female counterpart to Jesus. Other key teachings included auricular confession, celibacy as the ideal, lust as the root of all sin, and the goal of individual and communal perfection. The Shakers believed that they were a genuine expression of primitive Christianity and that truth was being ever revealed through their leadership and the communal spiritual experience. Although they disdained creedal formulations, they were concerned with theological expression and thus published numerous treatises, tracts, poems and articles explaining their beliefs and lifestyle.

Shaker lifestyle was simple, efficient and regulated, but not austere. A sacramental view of reality and a spirit of creativity resulted in many practical inventions and labor-saving devices. Children that members had brought in with them, as well as orphans and other children left with the Shakers, were included in the Shaker communities.

Some nineteen communities were formed, from Maine to Florida and west to Indiana and Kentucky. The central ministry was located in New Lebanon, New York. An exact count of membership is extremely difficult to make because of the frequent transfers between communities and fluidity of membership, but at its height it may have reached 5,000 members. Today there are a handful of Shaker women living in New Hampshire and Maine.

Six-Principle Baptists. An Arminian Baptist tradition maintaining the ordinance of the laying on of hands. In the seventeenth century, some English General Baptists had adopted Hebrews 6:1-2 as a six-point confessional standard: repentance, faith, baptism, laying on of hands, the resurrection of the dead and eternal life. But because the general assembly refused to adopt the Six Principles as its only official standard, Six-Principle Baptists separated and established their own assembly (1690). Their theology was Arminian, and they practiced closed communion.

Six-Principle Baptists appeared at an early date as minorities among the first Baptist churches in America—Providence and Newport—most of whose members were Calvinistic. By 1652 they had become the majority at Providence. By the 1670s several Rhode Island Six-Principle churches had formed what perhaps was the first Baptist association in America. In the 1940s three churches identified as Six-Principle Baptists listed 280 members, living mostly in Rhode Island and Pennsylvania.

Southern Baptist Convention. Largest Baptist body in the U.S. The Southern Baptist Convention (SBC) is composed of sixteen million baptized believers in about forty-two thousand churches in all fifty states of the U.S., making it the largest Protestant denomination in the U.S. Approximately half of all Baptists in the U.S. belong to churches affiliated with the Southern Baptist Convention.

The convention was organized on May 8, 1845, in Augusta, Georgia. Its separation from the Northern Baptists was due to issues arising out of the abolition movement in the U.S. Other factors, such as the freedom to carry on missionary activities without regard to the slavery issue and differences over the nature of denominational structure, were also contributing factors.

Theologically, most Southern Baptists are evangelicals and subscribe to the authority of the Bible in determining their ecclesiology and social action. They baptize by immersion believers who publicly profess faith; they hold that neither baptism nor the Lord's Supper convey sacramental grace. In their doctrine of salvation, Southern Baptists generally can be classified as modified Calvinists, being heirs of the Free Church tradition that includes both Calvinist and Arminian strains. Southern Baptists are not bound by a creed but share a confession of faith based on the New Hampshire Confession, first adopted by the Convention in 1925 and revised in 1963. Southern Baptist worship is nonliturgical. Preaching is central, while music constitutes an important element in the worship life of the churches.

Southern Baptists have steadfastly refused to join the National and World Councils of Churches. Its agencies, however, cooperate with various programs of the National Council of Churches on projects of mutual interest. Although not a member of the World Council of Churches, the Southern Baptist Convention took the lead in bringing disparate Baptist unions and conventions together into the Baptist World Alliance in 1905.

Southern Baptists jealously guard the autonomy of the local church. The local church is the highest judicature in Southern Baptist life. Yet the principle of cooperation commands the loyalty of most Southern Baptists. Local congregations are related to the SBC in the same way they are related to the state conventions and local associations, each of which is an autonomous body but closely interrelated. The state conventions sponsor educational and benevolent institutions, such as hospitals, orphanages and retirement villages, as well as mission programs, within their respective states.

The relationship between the congregations, the state convention and the SBC is voluntary. The SBC has no authority over the churches but is free to recommend and promote convention-wide programs. Without the cooperation and financial support of the local churches, the SBC could not function.

The work of the SBC is delegated to four boards, seven commissions and six seminaries. Responsibility for fifty-one colleges and six seminaries of the denomination is divided between the SBC, which sponsors the seminaries, and the state conventions, which operate the colleges and universities.

901 Commerce St.
Nashville, TN 37203
Phone: (615) 244-2355
Website: www.sbc.net

Swedenborgianism. *See* Church of the New Jerusalem.

Syrian Orthodox Church of Antioch. The Syrian Orthodox Church of Antioch participated in and fully accepted the teaching of Nicea (325), Constantinople (381) and Ephesus (431) but rejected the terminology of the Council of Chalcedon (451). Thus unlike Roman Catholic, Eastern Orthodox and Protestant churches, who believe Jesus Christ has two natures (divine and human), the Syrian Orthodox Church believes and confesses that Christ is of one nature and is indivisible into two separate natures, he being fully God and fully man in the unique oneness of his person and nature without mixture or confusion.

The presence of the Syrian Orthodox Church of Antioch in America dates back to the late nineteenth century, when religious persecution forced immigration from Ottoman Turkey to the U.S. They primarily settled in New Jersey, Massachusetts, Rhode Island and Detroit.

In the 1920s churches were built in west New York; Detroit; Worcester, Massachusetts; and Central Falls, Rhode Island. On November 15, 1957, Patriarch Ignatius Yacoub III officially established the Archdiocese of the Syrian Orthodox Church in the U.S. and Canada with His Eminence Archbishop Samuel as primate. On September 7, 1958, Archbishop Samuel consecrated a cathedral for the archdiocese in Hackensack (New Jersey). The 1960s saw new congre-gations organized in Los Angeles and Chicago. By the 1980s new parishes had been established in West Roxbury, Massachusetts;

Portland, Oregon; and California. There are presently 22 parishes and approximately 32,000 faithful served by 23 priests. The archdiocesan headquarters is presently located in Lodi, New Jersey.

The church is a member of both the World Council of Churches as well as the National Council of the Churches of Christ in the United States of America. Today, the seat of the Syrian Orthodox Patriarchate of Antioch is in Damascus, Syria.

Archdiocese of the Eastern USA
260 Elm Avenue
Teaneck, NJ 07666
Phone: (201) 801-0660; Fax: (201) 801-0603
Website: www.syrianorthodoxchurch.org

U

Ukrainian Catholics. Christians whose church is under the jurisdiction of the pope of Rome but whose church law is that of Eastern Orthodoxy. They are also called Ruthenian Catholics, Byzantine Rite Catholics or Uniates. The church's history began with the Union of Brest in 1596, when many Russian Orthodox churches within the expanding Polish kingdom agreed to accept Rome's authority in exchange for the right to retain their Orthodox practices, most notably the use of Slavonic instead of Latin in the liturgy and the tradition of allowing priests to be married.

In the late 1800s, people from these churches began to immigrate to the U.S. In North America, Ukrainian Catholics experienced considerable religious conflict. Latin rite Catholics tried to compel them to give up their Eastern traditions and follow Western ways. Eventually a papal decree in 1929 confirmed their right to maintain their distinct religious practices. After World War II, new emigration from Soviet-controlled territories increased their numbers.

There are more than 500,000 Eastern-Rite Catholics, mostly Ukranians and Ruthenians, in America. They are led by a metropolitan archbishop with his cathedral in Philadelphia and by annual synods of their bishops. Worldwide, Ukranian Catholics number over 4 million.

St. Nicholas Eparchy
2245 West Rice St.

Chicago, IL 60622
Phone: (773) 276-5080; Fax: (773) 276-6799
Website: catolicos.org

Unification Church (Moonies). A new religious movement founded in 1954. The founder of the Unification Church, the Reverend Sun Myung Moon, was born of Presbyterian parents in Korea, January 6, 1920. Although the movement's first American churches were established in the 1960s, it was during the 1970s that Moon first toured the U.S. and his group achieved visibility in the media as increasing numbers of young adults joined. Followers of Moon, popularly known as Moonies, became known for their zealous recruitment tactics and fund-raising efforts. Critics charged that the organization engaged in brainwashing and other authoritarian practices. Parents sometimes attempted to deprogram or coercively remove members from the group. Moonies claimed persecution by the press, the government and anticultists.

Moon's doctrine can be traced to a dramatic experience he claims took place on Easter morning in 1936 when Jesus appeared to him on a Korean mountainside and told him he was chosen to complete the earthly mission that Jesus failed to carry out fully. For the next nine years, Moon received a series of revelations which comprise the core of the movement's major book, *Divine Principle* (1966, 1973). According to Unification theology, restoration (salvation) will be accomplished by the Lord of the Second Advent, or Messiah, who will help unite all religions. Followers of Moon believe that he is that messenger of God. In order to pursue their religious goals and to achieve legitimation in the larger society, Unificationists founded a seminary in New York State, sponsor many ecumenical and academic conferences, and promote anti-Communist forums. The church is also involved in various publishing and business enterprises, including the *Washington Times*.

HSA-UWC, 4 West 43rd St.
New York, NY 10036
Website: www.unification.org

Union d'Eglises baptistes françaises au Canada (Union of French Baptist Churches in Canada). *See* Canadian Baptist Ministries.

Unitarian Universalist Association. The Unitarian Universalist Association (UUA) was established in 1961 with the merger of the American Unitarian Association and the Universalist Church of America. Both were small denominations, primarily of New England origin, that exemplified two separate courses of the development of religious liberalism in America.

Unitarianism refers most generally to a belief that God is one Person rather than a Trinity. American Unitarianism had its most immediate origins among a group of mid-eighteenth-century Boston-area clergy who became skeptical both of the revivalism of the Great Awakening and also of traditional Puritan Calvinism. These men, led by Charles Chauncy, Ebenezer Gay and Jonathan Mayhew, were New England Arminians who were especially hostile to the doctrine of original sin. The first open rejection of the doctrine of the Trinity, however, came not from them but from Boston's Anglican King's Chapel, which in 1785 prepared an edition of the Book of Common Prayer devoid of trinitarian references.

Although the Boston liberals did not wish to break formally with Puritan Congregationalism, their hand was forced by conservatives such as Jedidiah Morse, who precipitated the first Unitarian controversy during the early decades of the nineteenth century. The appointment of the liberal Henry Ware as Hollis Professor at Harvard in 1805 was a major victory. William Ellery Channing, the movement's most eloquent spokesman, outlined the liberal position publicly in his Baltimore sermon of 1819. In 1825 the rift between factions of Congregationalists had become irreconcilable. The American Unitarian Association was founded in Boston as a loose institutional alliance of liberals and included eighty-eight of the hundred oldest congregations in eastern Massachusetts.

Meanwhile, another liberal movement was taking shape, not in cosmopolitan Boston, but primarily in smaller towns along the Atlantic coast. Universalism, the doctrine that all of humanity would ultimately be saved, was first preached in New England by John Murray. In Philadelphia a "Society of Universal Baptists" was founded by Elhanan Winchester and based on a similar optimistic message. Universalism was soon given systematic theological articulation and leadership through the work of Hosea Ballou in writings such as his *Treatise on the Atonement* (1805) and his ministry in Boston. Although the movement resisted tight organization, legal pressures led to the forming of the Universalist Church of America in 1833. The denomination found its greatest strength in small towns and rural areas, expanding from its bases in New England and the Mid-Atlantic States into the South and beyond. Its maximum strength, attained around the turn of the twentieth century, was about 65,000.

By the twentieth century the appeal of the two denominations had been challenged by several factors. Such traditional liberal ideas as the benevolence of God, the exemplary character of Jesus and the possibilities for human growth through personal moral cultivation had become widely accepted through the spread of Protestant liberalism in many seminaries and pulpits. Both Unitarians and Universalists also faced the question of coming to terms with the nontheistic humanist movement within their own ranks, and were further undermined by administrative problems and the financial impact of the Great Depression.

The two denominations merged in 1961 to form the Unitarian-Universalist Association. Its headquarters are in Boston, and it recognizes three seminaries: Harvard (interdenominational), Meadville-Lombard in Chicago and Starr King in Berkeley. Polity is congregational, with a national board of trustees composed of delegates from twenty-three districts in the U.S. and Canada, and others elected at large. Membership in the early 2000s stood at about 158,000, with approximately 1,000 churches and fellowships and 1,600 clergy. The UUA is vocal in its commitment to progressive social issues, including environmentalism, feminism and gay rights. It imposes no creedal tests and recognizes its roots both in the Judeo-Christian tradition as well as in humanistic sources. Although New England remains a bastion of numerical strength, Unitarian Universalists can be found throughout the nation, especially in urban areas, academic communities and "high tech" centers.

25 Beacon St.
Boston, MA 02108
Phone: (617) 742-2100
Website: www.uua.org

United Brethren in Christ. *See* Church of the United Brethren in Christ.

United Church of Canada. Canada's largest Protestant denomination. The United Church of Canada was formed officially on June 10, 1925, out of the union of the Methodist Church, Canada (representing the large majority of Canadian Methodists); the Congregational Union of Canada (representing virtually all Canadian Congregationalists); the Council of Local Union Churches (numbering about 3,000 relatively small congregations); and about two-thirds of the *Presbyterian Church in Canada.

The union capped several decades of negotiations among these churches. The resulting denomination was the first modern church in the world fully to unite such diverse traditions in one religious body. The church later was augmented by the additions of the Wesleyan Methodist Church of Bermuda (1930) and the Canada Conference of the Evangelical United Brethren (1968).

The church's polity combines elements from the constituent churches, but most resembles Presbyterianism. The church is governed by a General Council that meets every two years. A moderator, elected for the same period, directs the General Council and represents the church between councils. The secretary of the General Council holds the other most important administrative post. The various ministries of the church are centralized under boards and administrators in Toronto, but the boards are duplicated at the conference, presbytery and, often, individual church levels. Church courts are also established at the conference and presbytery levels. An official board, chaired by the pastor, combines the session and board of stewards in the local church.

The United Church's "Basis of Union" set forth a statement of faith that agreed with the basic evangelical doctrines held in common by its constituent traditions, but the church also took in a large number of the most influential Canadian liberal theologians and church leaders of the time. Since then its leadership, including its theological seminaries, has been characterized generally by liberal or neo-orthodox theology and a strong commitment to social issues and the mainline ecumenical movement. The Renewal Fellowship, composed of a number of evangelicals within the church, has sought generally to influence the church away from what it sees to be unorthodox theology.

The United Church is a member of the World Methodist Council, the World Alliance of Reformed Churches and the Canadian and World Councils of Churches. Declining in numbers since the early 1960s, the church claimed over 3,600 congregations, over 637,000 adult members and over 1.5 million affiliated Canadians in the early 2000s.

3250 Bloor Street West, Suite 300
Toronto, Ontario M8X 2Y4
Phone: (416) 231-5931; Fax: (416) 231-3103
Website: www.united-church.ca

United Church of Christ. Formed in 1957, the United Church of Christ (UCC) was a merger of the Congregational Christian Churches and the Evangelical and Reformed Church. Through its denominational traditions the Congregational wing of the UCC goes back to the original Congregationalism of Puritan New England. Although Congregationalists joined forces in creating the American Board of Commissioners for Foreign Mission (1812) and the American Missionary Association (1846), it was not until 1871 that Congregationalists founded the National Council of Congregational Churches (NCCC). In 1892 the NCCC was joined by a body of Congregational Methodist churches in Georgia and Alabama, and in 1925 the Evangelical Protestant Churches, a group of Ohio Valley congregations, also joined the NCCC.

In 1931 the General Convention of the Christian Church, or Christian Connection, united with the NCCC to form the General Council of Congregational and Christian Churches. The General Convention of the Christian Church, a body arising from the nineteenth-century Restoration Movement, had been seeking union with other Protestant churches since 1924.

The other church tradition represented in the UCC union of 1957, the Evangelical and Reformed Church, was itself the product of a union of two church traditions, both of them tracing their histories back to German immigrants to America. On the one hand the General Synod of the Reformed Church in the United States (a name they adopted in 1863) had originated in the organizing efforts of John

Philip Boehm and Michael Schlatter, who organized German Reformed congregations in Pennsylvania in the early 1700s and formed their first coetus in 1747 under the jurisdiction of the Dutch Reformed Church. The other member of this 1934 union, the Evangelical Synod of North America, was a product of several Midwestern immigrant congregations of the Evangelical Union of Prussia, itself a German Lutheran and Reformed amalgamation brought about by King Frederick William III (1770-1840). The Evangelical Synod and the Reformed Church began exploring their common ground in the late 1920s, finally becoming one denomination on June 26, 1934.

The General Council of the Congregational Christian Churches and the Evangelical and Reformed Church began exploring the possibilities of union in the early 1940s, a process that concluded in the birth of the UCC at a meeting in Cleveland, Ohio, on June 25-27, 1957. Its theological spectrum encompasses churches and individuals ranging from liberal to moderately evangelical. Its national and conference leadership would be classified as predominantly liberal in theology. Evangelical renewal efforts since the 1970s have resulted in a conservative (UCC People for Biblical Witness) and a charismatic fellowship (Fellowship of Charismatic Christians in the UCC). In the 1980s, concern for theological revitalization has brought about the Biblical Witness Fellowship and the Biblical-Theological-Liturgical Group.

The contemporary UCC denomination is noted for its social consciousness, having been influenced by the Social Gospel Movement of the early twentieth century. It seeks to work for peace, the slowing of the arms race, human rights, women's rights and gay rights. Local church autonomy, the vocation of all believers and ecumenism continue to characterize the UCC. In the early 2000s the UCC reported an inclusive membership of 1,359,105 in 5,888 congregations throughout the United States.

700 Prospect Avenue
Cleveland, OH 44115
Phone: (216) 736-2100
Website: www.ucc.org

United Holy Church of America. A predominantly African American Holiness denomination. The United Holy Church of America

was founded on May 1, 1886, in Method, a suburb of Raleigh, North
Carolina. The chief purpose of the early meetings was to seek the
"deeper life of sanctification" and recover the lost zeal of the mainline evangelical churches. A trinitarian body, it accepts the faith con-
fessed in the Apostles' Creed and delimited by the Protestant Reformation. Tremendous emphasis is placed on sanctification as
essential for Christian life. Equal emphasis is placed on Spirit baptism, which, like sanctification, is regarded as subsequent to conversion. The United Holy Church practices charismatic manifestations
of the Spirit, including speaking in tongues. The Church does not,
however, insist on speaking in tongues as the "necessary evidence"
of Spirit baptism.

This Holiness church emerged during a period when lynching,
dire poverty, racial segregation and limited educational opportuni-
ties affected the lives of African Americans. The Church responded
with an emphasis on holiness that preserved a focus on inner-trans-
formation and high scriptural standards for ethics. Spiritual em-
powerment was the source for holy living, and a prophetic social
consciousness judged the culture and kept the cause of the dispos-
sessed foremost in the practical programs of the church.

The church experienced unsurpassed growth in the first half of
the twentieth century through a program of evangelism and missions centered in district convocations. In 1993 the church reported
50,000 members in 470 churches. The greatest concentration of
membership remains along the East Coast, and the present headquarters are located in Greensboro, North Carolina.

5104 Dunstan Rd.
Greensboro, NC 27405
Phone: (336) 621-0669
Website: http://members.aol.com/newpent/npchca.htm

United Methodist Church. The United Methodist Church came into
existence in 1968 through a union between the Methodist Church
and the Evangelical United Brethren—two denominations that
traced their roots to revivals in eighteenth-century Britain and
America.

The name *Methodist* originated as a satirical allusion to the order
and regularity of behavior in the Holy Club to which John Wesley

belonged as a student at Oxford University. Wesley retained it as a name for the societies, classes and bands that he began to organize in 1739 within the Church of England to provide worship, discipline and nurture for the converts attracted by his evangelistic sermons. Wesley encouraged a devotion that blended confidence in justification by grace with a commitment to a holiness that could, by God's grace, find its fulfillment in the perfecting of love.

In 1769 the British conference, under Wesley's leadership, officially sent missionaries to America. Two years later it sent Francis Asbury, who helped direct a revival that by 1784 had attracted 14,988 members under the care of eighty-four itinerant preachers and numerous lay class leaders.

In 1784 Wesley agreed to ordain elders and set apart Asbury and Thomas Coke as "superintendents" of the Methodists in America. On December 24, the American preachers convened for the "Christmas Conference" in Baltimore to form the Methodist Episcopal Church.

After 1784 the Methodist Episcopal Church grew especially through the agency of circuit riders, who traveled on horseback to organize classes and congregations on the frontier, and of camp meetings, which maintained the revivalist zeal. It benefited also from a disciplined ministry: bishops assigned the itinerant preachers to their circuits. By 1840 the Methodist Episcopal Church, with 580,098 members, was the largest Protestant denomination in America.

Growth continued even after debate over slavery divided the denomination in 1844, but after the Civil War the Northern Church outstripped its Southern counterpart. By 1880 it could boast 1,743,000 members, compared to 848,000 in the Methodist Episcopal Church, South, which had suffered the loss of 158,964 African American members after emancipation. Increasingly, new Methodists came from the middle classes, and the new members began to demand an educated ministry and more refined styles of worship.

In 1939 the two regional churches, along with the Methodist Protestant Church, reunited as the Methodist Church. Seven years later, when the church of the United Brethren in Christ and the Evangelical Church joined together as the Evangelical United Brethren Church. G. Bromley Oxnam, a Methodist bishop, suggested a further merger, which was realized in 1968 at a uniting conference in Dallas. Delegates for the 800,000 Evangelical United Brethren members joined with representatives of ten million Methodists to form the United Methodist Church. Their current membership is 8,340,000 in 35,469 churches.

General Commission on Communications
P.O. Box 320
Nashville, TN 37202-0320
Phone: (615) 742-5410; Fax: (615) 742-5415
Website: www.umc.org

United Pentecostal Church, International. Oneness Pentecostal denomination. Formed in 1945 by the merger of the Pentecostal Assemblies of Jesus Christ and the Pentecostal Church, Inc., the United Pentecostal Church is the largest white oneness Pentecostal denomination. Its two constituent bodies had separated from the Pentecostal Assemblies of the World in 1924 in a secession in part motivated by racial tension. Earlier, some of its prominent leaders had left the Assemblies of God in a 1916 dispute over the baptismal formula and the nature of the Godhead. The group's doctrinal distinctives include the insistence that water baptism by immersion must be administered "in the name of Jesus" and the belief that there is only one Person in the Godhead, Jesus Christ. As with the Assemblies of God, they hold to the "finished work of grace," believing that sanctification begins at conversion and progresses toward perfection throughout one's lifetime. The denomination endorses a more rigorous social behavior code than do white trinitarian Pentecostal denominations of similar size. In 2002 there were 4,142 congregations with an inclusive membership of approximately 500,000. The denomination supports over five hundred missionaries in more than one hundred countries. The UPCI is located in more than 170 countries with a worldwide constituency of more than four million.

8855 Dunn Rd.
Hazelwood, MO 63042
Phone: (314) 837-7300; Fax: (314) 837-4503
Website: www.umc.org

Unity School of Christianity. A New Thought religious movement. The Unity School of Christianity traces its origin to Kansas City, Missouri, where, in 1889, its cofounders, Myrtle and Charles Fillmore, decided to dedicate their lives to the study and teaching of practical Christianity. From modest beginnings, Unity has grown in size and impact so that today it daily affects the lives of over two million people through its devotional magazine, *The Daily Word.* The Unity movement, through the representation of the Association of Unity Churches (a closely affiliated institution), has 525 field ministries and 275 affiliated study groups. More than 400,000 people receive its monthly denominational magazine, *Unity,* and over two-and-a-half million contact its prayer ministry, Silent Unity, annually. It is by far the largest segment of the New Thought family, while also being unique among New Thought groups in its emphatic claim to be a Christian movement. Unity School is located at Unity Village, just outside of Kansas City, Missouri.

Unity has discernible theological and historical links with Christian Science that can be traced through the influence of E. B. Weeks on the Fillmores. In 1886 Weeks, a disciple of Emma Curtis Hopkins (who had broken ties with Mary Baker Eddy), was lecturing in Kansas City on mental healing. The Fillmores attended one of the lectures, and as a result Myrtle began a process of healing that by 1888 resulted in a complete healing of her lifelong tuberculosis.

Myrtle's healing precipitated the Fillmores' interest in New Thought, which eventuated in the founding of Unity. Originally established as a healing and publication ministry, Unity soon assumed a sectarian character. Although Unity is nondoctrinal, several foundational teachings are notable: (1) the absolute goodness of God and the unreality of evil, (2) the innate divinity of humanity, (3) the creative nature of consciousness, (4) the freedom of individuals in matters of belief and (5) the acceptance of spiritually interpreted Christian doctrine as normative. Unity's distinctive symbol is a winged globe.

V

Vineyard USA. *See* Association of Vineyard Churches.

W

Watchtower Bible and Tract Society. *See* Jehovah's Witnesses.

Way International, The. Religious group founded on the teachings of Victor Paul Wierwille. The Way International began in the 1940s under Wierwille's radio ministry and assumed its current name in 1974. The movement experienced dramatic growth during the Jesus People era of the late 1960s and continued to expand in the 1970s under Wierwille's leadership. Since his death in 1985, the organization has declined.

Wierwille, formerly a pastor in the Evangelical and Reformed Church (now *United Church of Christ), received a degree from Princeton Theological Seminary in 1941 and was later awarded a doctorate from an unaccredited correspondence school. In 1953 he developed the first Power for Abundant Living class, which became the cornerstone and chief recruitment device of The Way International. The organization is headquartered in New Knoxville, Ohio, and operates The Way College in Emporia, Kansas. Many members participate in The Way Corps, a four-year leadership-training program. Known for their aggressive friendship evangelism and spiritual elitism, The Way does not consider itself a church or denomination but prefers to be known as a biblical research and teaching organization. Its belief system derives largely from the writing and teaching of Wierwille, who believed that God spoke to him audibly and gave him the only correct interpretation of Scripture since the first century. Wierwille's views depart from traditional orthodox Christianity at a number of points. He denied the deity of Jesus Christ and rejected the doctrine of the Trinity. He also denied the distinct personhood of the Holy Spirit and taught that speaking in tongues is the necessary sign that a person has been born again. As of 2002 there are some 58,000 members in 870 churches in about 90 nations.

P.O. Box 328
New Knoxville, OH 45871
Website: www.theway.com

Wesleyan Church. A Holiness denomination. The Wesleyan Church was formed on June 26, 1968, through the union of the Wesleyan Methodist Church and the Pilgrim Holiness Church. Both bodies had a theological kinship in their acceptance of the Wesleyan tradition as it had been transformed through the Holiness Movement of the late-nineteenth century.

The Wesleyan Methodist Church was organized in 1843 by abolitionist clergy and lay people who had been protesting the tolerance of slavery by the Methodist Episcopal Church. When Methodist bishops sought to silence them, twenty-two ministers and 6,000 members left the denomination and formed the Wesleyan Methodist Connection of America. This took place only one year before the historic split between the Methodist Episcopal Church and the Methodist Episcopal Church, South. The new denomination was also opposed to what it perceived to be abuses of the episcopacy in the mother denomination and drew up an ecclesiastical structure that included lay participation in the annual conference and the election of a president instead of a bishop. The Connection also opposed the use of tobacco and alcohol, participation in secret societies and immodest dress. The body did not consider its differences with mainstream Methodism to be reconciled after the Civil War, and in the latter half of the nineteenth century it was deeply influenced by the Holiness Movement. In 1947 it changed its name to the Wesleyan Methodist Church.

The Pilgrim Holiness Church was a product of the Holiness Movement, originating as the International Holiness Union and Prayer League in 1897 in Cincinnati, Ohio. This movement, formed around holiness, healing, evangelism and premillennialism, had grown into a denomination by 1913 and through several mergers with like-minded bodies became the Pilgrim Holiness Church in 1922.

The denomination has maintained a strong emphasis on foreign missions and now has churches established in thirty-four countries outside of the U.S. and Canada. Membership in the U.S. numbers more than 114,000 with an additional 5,800 in Canada. The denomination maintains membership in the Christian Holiness Association, the National Association of Evangelicals and the World Methodist Council. Its educational institutions include Houghton College in Houghton, New York, and Marion College in Marion, Indiana

P.O. Box 50434
Indianapolis, IN 46250
Phone: (317) 570-5100
Website: www.wesleyan.org

Willow Creek Association. The Willow Creek Association (WCA)

was launched in 1992 to build a global network of like-minded churches around the model and values of Willow Creek Community Church, an evangelical megachurch founded in 1975 in suburban Chicago. Willow Creek Community Church is known for championing "seeker sensitivity" in its services and outreach efforts.

The WCA's goal "is to equip members with vision, training, and resources to build thriving, biblically functioning churches." Within ten years, membership in the association grew to more than 9,500 churches in 25 countries, with annual attendance of more than 100,000 at various WCA conferences and training events.

Though WCA is not a denomination (WCA churches hale from ninety denominations), member churches must affirm an evangelical and orthodox statement of faith.

P.O. Box 3188
Barrington, IL 60011-3188
Phone: (847) 765-0070; Fax: (847) 765-5046
Website: www.willowcreek.com

Wisconsin Evangelical Lutheran Synod. Conservative Lutheran denomination. Clergy commissioned in Europe by the Langenberg Mission Society to minister to scattered German Lutheran and Reformed immigrants in America founded the Wisconsin Evangelical Lutheran Synod (WELS) in 1850. Chief among these founders was John Muehlhaeuser (1804-1868), the Synod's first president. In 1878 the denomination established a theological seminary, which in 1917 was moved from Milwaukee to suburban Wauwatosa and subsequently relocated to Mequon, Wisconsin. Further progress toward denominational status occurred in 1892 when the Synod joined forces with the synods of Minnesota and Michigan for the purpose of cooperation in education and mission work. The members of this federation were amalgamated into the Joint Synod of Wisconsin and Other States in 1917.

Historically, the Wisconsin Synod has moved from a weak confessionalism to a more staunchly conservative Lutheran stance. Set in the 1860s by John Bading (1824-1913) and Adolf Hoenecke (1835-1908), both of whom insisted on stricter allegiance to the Lutheran confessions and a less tolerant attitude regarding altar and pulpit fellowship, this trend was reinforced by closer ties with

the Lutheran Church—Missouri Synod in the Evangelical Lutheran Synodical Conference (1872). It was solidified by controversy
during the late 1920s when the Synod resisted its own less dog-
matic "Wauwatosa Theology" and expelled John Philipp Koehler
(1859-1951) from teaching. Charges of "unionism" directed at the
Missouri Synod following World War II led in 1963 to withdrawal
from the Synodical Conference.

In the early 2000s the Wisconsin Synod numbered 401,615 baptized members in 1,228 North American congregations, with headquarters in Milwaukee, Wisconsin.

2929 N. Mayfair Road
Milwaukee, WI 53222
Phone: (414) 256-3888; Fax: (414) 256-3899
Website: www.wels.net

Worldwide Church of God. An evangelical denomination that was
formerly an adventist sect. The founder of the Worldwide Church of
God (WCG), Herbert W. Armstrong, was ordained in 1931 by the Oregon Conference of the *Church of God (Seventh-Day). In 1934 Armstrong, while still associated with the Church of God, began a radio
ministry called the Radio Church of God and began publishing *The
Plain Truth*. A devoted student of the Bible, Armstrong had by this
time come to believe in British Israelism. This doctrine, which identifies the ten lost tribes of Israel with Anglo-Saxons, became part of
his church's larger complex of beliefs that included an emphasis on
Old Testament law and the observance of Jewish festivals.

By 1937 Armstrong had withdrawn from the Church of God
(Seventh-Day). His own following grew, and in 1947 he moved his
headquarters to Pasadena, California, where he founded Ambassador College. There the movement continued to prosper, with the radio broadcast, followed by a television ministry, reaching an ever-
widening audience. By 1974 distribution of *The Plain Truth* had
reached 2 million.

The group suffered losses during the 1970s. Schisms among
members, alleged scandalous conduct by the leadership and a law-
suit brought against the church shook the organization. Theological
dispute also played a significant role. When Armstrong's prediction
of an eschatological event of cosmic magnitude failed to occur in

1972, many members were disappointed. But by the mid-1980s the church had stabilized and was once again growing.

Before Armstrong died in 1986, he appointed Joseph Tkach Sr. as his successor. Along with some WCG pastors, Tkach began to examine, modify or drop some of Armstrong's unorthodox teachings. In 1993 the WCG officially accepted the doctrine of the Trinity, and in the following years the church dropped its adherence to British Israelitism and declared that its members did not have to abide by the Old Testament laws and festivals to be faithful to Christ. The transition was so complete that in 1997 the WCG was accepted as a full member of the National Association of Evangelicals.

This great upheaval has been costly to the denomination. Circulation of *The Plain Truth* has dropped from 8,000,000 to 100,000, the TV ministry is gone, Ambassador College has closed, the church's Pasadena properties are being sold, and hundreds of employees have been laid off. Tens of thousands of members withdrew from the denomination and formed new churches faithful to Armstrong's teachings. In 2003 WCG had about 58,000 members worshiping in 870 congregations in 90 countries. (About half of the congregations are in the U.S.)

300 West Green Street
Pasadena, CA 91123
Phone: (800) 309-4466
Website: www.wcg.org

List of Contributors

Most of the entries in this dictionary are adapted from the *Dictionary of Christianity in America*, edited by Daniel G. Reid, Robert D. Linder, Bruce L. Shelley and Harry S. Stout. New entries are indicated in the list of contributors by a dagger (†) next to the contributor's name.

Aivazian, Arshen A., Parish Priest, St. Paul Armenian Church, Fresno, California: *Armenian Church*

†Blankman, Drew, Associate Editor, InterVarsity Press, Downers Grove, Illinois: *Association of Vineyard Churches; Evangelical Presbyterian Church*

Blumhofer, Edith L., Project Director, Institute for the Study of American Evangelicals; Professor of History, Wheaton College, Wheaton, Illinois: *Assemblies of God; United Pentecostal Church, International*

Brackney, William H., Professor of Church History, Baylor University, Waco, Texas: *American Baptist Church in the USA*

Bratt, James D., Director, Calvin Center for Christian Scholarship, Calvin College, Grand Rapids, Michigan: *Christian Reformed Church in North America*

Bruins, Elton J., Evert J. and Hattie E. Blekkink Professor Emeritus of Religion, Hope College, Holland, Michigan: *Reformed Church in America*

Chilton, Roger H., Rector, St. Swithun's Anglican Church, Pymble, NSW, Australia: *Anglican Church of Canada*

Clouse, Robert G., Professor of History, Indiana State University, Terre Haute, Indiana: *Fellowship of Grace Brethren Churches*

De Chant, Dell, Instructor in Religious Studies and Undergraduate Director, University of South Florida, Tampa, Florida: *Liberal Catholic Church; Unity School of Christianity*

Diefenthaler, Jon T., President, Southeastern District, Lutheran Church—Missouri Synod: *Wisconsin Evangelical Lutheran Synod*

Durnbaugh, Donald F., retired Professor of Religion and History, Elizabethtown College, Elizabethtown, Pennsylvania: *Church of the Brethren*

Edwards, Lillie J., Director of African-American and African Studies, Drew University, Madison, New Jersey: *African Methodist Episcopal Church; African Methodist Episcopal Zion Church*

Eller, David B., Professor of Religion, Elizabethtown College, Elizabethtown, Pennsylvania: *Amana Church Society; Hutterian Brethren (Hutterites); Schwenkfelders*

Ellis, Walter E., Senior Minister, Fairview Baptist Church, Vancouver, British Columbia: *Canadian Baptist Ministries; Christian Church (Disciples of Christ) in Canada Doukhobors*

Enns-Rempel, Kevin M., Archivist and History Faculty, Fresno Pacific University, Fresno, California: *Fellowship of Evangelical Bible Churches; General Conference of Mennonite Brethren Churches of North America*

Enroth, Ronald M., Professor of Sociology, Westmont College, Santa Barbara, California: *The Family; Unification Church; The Way International*

Estep, William R., Distinguished Professor of Church History Emeritus, Chairman of the Historical Division, School of Theology, Southwestern Baptist Theological Seminary, Fort Worth, Texas: *Southern Baptist Convention*

Evans, William B., Associate Professor of Bible and Religion, Eskine College, Due West, South Carolina: *Cumberland Presbyterian Church*

FitzGerald, Thomas, Professor of Church History and Historical Theology, Holy Cross Greek Orthodox School of Theology, Brookline, Massachusetts: *Autocephalous Orthodox Church; Greek Orthodox Archdiocese of North and South America, Orthodox Church in America*

Frank, Albert H., Adjunct Professor, Moravian Theological Seminary, Bethlehem, Pennsylvania: *Moravian Church in America*

Freundt, Albert H., Jr., Professor of Church History, Emeritus, Reformed Theological Seminary, Jackson, Mississippi: *Presbyterian Church in America*

Graham, Stephen R., Dean of Faculty and Academic Life, Professor of American Church History, North Park Theological Seminary, Chicago, Illinois: *Evangelical Covenant Church of America*

Gravely, William B., Professor Emeritus of Religious Studies, University of Denver, Denver, Colorado: *Christian Methodist Episcopal Church*

Gross, Leonard, Consulting Archivist, Archives of the Mennonite Church U.S.A., Goshen, Indiana: *Amish, Old Order; Mennonite Church/ (Old) Mennonite Church*

Guelzo, Allen C., Grace Kea Professor of History, Eastern University, St. Davids, Pennsylvania: *Reformed Episcopal Church*

Hall, Cline E., Associate Professor, History Department, Liberty University, Lynchburg, Virginia: *Independent Fundamental Churches of America*

Hall, Joseph H., retired Professor of Church History and Librarian, Mid-America Reformed Seminary, Dyer, Indiana: *Bible Presbyterian Churches; General Synod of the Association of Reformed Presbyterian Church; Reformed Presbyterian Church in North America*

Hanson, Calvin B., retired Director of Internship, Trinity Evangelical Divinity School, Deerfield, Illinois: *Evangelical Free Church of America*

Hennesey, James, Professor of the History of Christianity, Canisius College, Buffalo, New York: *Roman Catholicism*

Hexham, Irving, Professor of Religious Studies, University of Calgary, Calgary, Alberta: *Church of Jesus Christ of Latter Day Saints; Jehovah's Witnesses*

Holifield, E. Brooks, Charles Howard Candler Professor of American Church History, Candler School of Theology, Emory University, Atlanta, Georgia: *United Methodist Church*

Hollinger, Dennis P., Dean of College Ministries and College Pastor, Professor of Christian Ethics, Messiah College, Grantham, Pennsylvania: *Christian and Missionary Alliance*

Johnson, James E., Professor of History and Department Chair, Bethel College, St. Paul, Minnesota: *Baptist General Conference*

Juhnke, James C., Professor of History, Bethel College, North Newton, Kansas: *General Conference Mennonite Church*

Kolb, Robert A., Mission Professor of Systematic Theology and Director of the Institute for Mission Studies, Concordia Seminary, St. Louis, Missouri: *Lutheran Church—Missouri Synod*

Land, Gary G., Professor, Chairman, Department of History, Andrews University, Berrien Springs, Michigan: *Seventh-day Adventists*

Logan, Samuel T., Jr., President and Professor of Church History, Westminster Theological Seminary, Philadelphia, Pennsylvania: *Orthodox Presbyterian Church*

McBeth, H. Leon, Distinguished Professor of Church History, Southwestern Baptist Theological Seminary, Fort Worth, Texas: *Free Will Baptists*

McKinley, Edward H., Professor of History, Asbury College, Wilmore, Kentucky: *The Salvation Army*

Meno, Chorepiscopus John P., General Secretary of the Archdiocese of the Syrian Orthodox Church in the United States and Canada; Dean of St. Mark's Syrian Orthodox Cathedral, Hackensack, New Jersey: *Syrian Orthodox Church of Antioch*

Mercadante, Linda A., B. Robert Straker Chair in Historical Theology, Methodist Theological School, Delaware, Ohio: *Shakers*

Miethe, Terry L., Dean and Professor of Philosophy and Theology for the Oxford Study Centre, Oxford, England, and Lynchburg, Virginia: *Christian Church (Disciples of Christ); Christian Churches/Churches of Christ (Independent)*

Olbricht, Thomas H., Professor Emeritus, Pepperdine University, Malibu, California: *Churches of Christ (Non-Instrumental)*

Raser, Harold E., Professor of the History of Christianity, Nazarene Theological Seminary, Kansas City, Missouri: *Church of the Nazarene*

Reid, Daniel G., Robert D. Linder, Bruce L. Shelley, Harry S. Stout, Editors of the *Dictionary of Christianity in America: Association of Evangelical Lutheran Churches; Evangelical Friends International; Evangelical Lutheran Church in America; Wesleyan Church; Worldwide Church of God*

Rennie, Ian S., Vice President and Academic Dean (retired), Ontario Theological Seminary, Willowdale, Ontario: *Associated Gospel Church; Evangelical Lutheran Church in Canada; Pentecostal Assemblies of Canada*

Sable, Thomas F., Associate Professor of Theology, University of Scranton, Scranton, Pennsylvania: *Eastern-Rite Catholics; Maronite Catholics, Melchite Catholics*

Schoepflin, Rennie B., Associate Professor of History and Chair in the Department of History, Politics, and Society at La Sierra University, Riverside, California: *Church of Christ, Scientist*

Scott, Stephen E., Writer-Researcher, People's Place, Columbia, Pennsylvania: *Old Order River Brethren*

Selleck, Ronald E., Professor of Theology, Houghton Graduate School of Theology, High Point, North Carolina: *Friends, Religious Society of (Quakers); Friends General Conference (Hicksites)*

Shelley, Bruce L., Senior Professor of Church History and Historical Theology, Denver Seminary, Denver, Colorado: *Conservative Baptist Association of America*

Sider, E. Morris, Professor Emeritus of History and English Literature, Messiah College, Grantham, Pennsylvania: *Brethren in Christ Church*

Spivey, James T., Jr., Associate Professor of Church History, Southwestern Baptist Theological Seminary, Fort Worth, Texas: *General Association of Regular Baptist Churches; General Baptists; Missionary Baptists; Particular Baptists; Primitive Baptists; Regular Baptists; Separate Baptists; Seventh-day Baptists; Six-Principle Baptists*

Stackhouse, John G., Jr., Sangwoo Youtong Chee Chair of Theology and Culture at Regent College, Vancouver, British Columbia: *Plymouth Brethren; Presbyterian Church in Canada; The United Church of Canada*

Stanley, Susie C., Professor of Historical Theology and Executive Director of the Wesleyan/Holiness Women Clergy International, Messiah College, Grantham, Pennsylvania: *Church of God (Anderson, Indiana); Church of God (Cleveland, Tennessee); Church of God in Christ; Church of God of Prophecy; Church of God (Seventh Day)*

Steeves, Paul D., Professor of History and Director of Russian Studies, Stetson University, DeLand, Florida: *Ukrainian Catholics*

Strege, Merle D., Chair, Department of Religious Studies and Professor of Historical Theology, School of Theology, Anderson University, Anderson, Indiana: *Christian Holiness Association*

Towns, Elmer L., Dean, School of Religion, Liberty University, Lynchburg, Virginia: *Fundamentalist Baptist Fellowship*

Turner, William C., Jr., Associate Professor of the Practice of Homiletics, Duke University Divinity School, Durham, North Carolina: *United Holy Church of America*

Vos, Howard F., Emeritus Professor of History and Archaeology, The King's College, Tuxedo, New York: *Church of the New Jerusalem; The Church of the United Brethren in Christ*

Warner, Wayne E., Director, Flower Pentecostal Heritage Center, Springfield, Missouri: *International Church of the Foursquare Gospel*

Weaver, C. Douglas, Barney Averitt Chair of Christianity, Brewton-Parker College, Mount Vernon, Georgia: *American Baptist Association*

Webber, Robert E., William R. and Geraldyn B. Myers Professor of Ministry, Northern Baptist Theological Seminary, Lombard, Illinois: *Protestant Episcopal Church in the USA*

Weeks, Louis B., President and Professor of Historical Theology in the Walter W. Moore and Charles E. S. Kraemer Presidential Chairs, Union Theological Seminary and Presbyterian School of Christian Education, Richmond, Virginia: *Presbyterian Church (USA)*

Wenger, J. C., Professor Emeritus of Historical Theology, Goshen Biblical Seminary, Elkhart, Indiana: *Church of God in Christ, Mennonite*

White, Charles E., Professor of Christian Thought and History, Spring

Arbor University, Spring Arbor, Michigan: *Free Methodist Church of North America*

Whiteman, Curtis W., Professor of Historical Theology, Westmont College, Santa Barbara, California: *Baptist Bible Union*

Williams, Peter W., Distinguished Professor of Religion and American Studies and Director of the Program in American Studies, Miami University, Oxford, Ohio: *Unitarian Universalist Association*

Wilshire, Leland E., Professor of History, Biola University, La Mirada, California: *Conservative Congregational Christian Church; United Church of Christ*

Wilt, Paul C., retired Professor of History, Westmont College, Santa Barbara, California: *Bible Church Movement*

†Zimmerman, David, Associate Editor, InterVarsity Press, Downers Grove, Illinois: *Willow Creek Association*

Index

Six-Principle Baptists
Southern Baptist Convention

Brethren Churches
See Anabaptist/Brethren/
  Mennonite Churches

Canadian Churches
Anglican Church of Canada
Baptist Convention of Ontario
  and Quebec. *See* Canadian
  Baptist Ministries
Baptist Union of Western
  Canada. *See* Canadian Baptist
  Ministries
Canadian Baptist Ministries
Church of Christ (Disciples of
  Christ) in Canada
Convention of Atlantic Baptist
  Churches. *See* Canadian Baptist
  Ministries
Doukhobors (Dukhobors)
Evangelical Lutheran Church in
  Canada
Pentecostal Church of Canada
Presbyterian Church in Canada
*Union d'Eglise baptistes françaises
au Canada* (Union of French
  Baptist Churches in Canada).
  See Canadian Baptist Ministries
United Church of Canada

Charismatic Churches
Association of Vineyard Churches

Eastern Orthodox Churches
Armenian Church
Greek Orthodox Archdiocese of
  North and South America
Orthodox Church in America
Syrian Orthodox Church of
  Antioch

Eastern-Rite Catholic Churches
Marionite Catholics
Melchite Greek Catholic Church
Ukrainian Catholics

**Evangelical/Independent/Free
Churches**
Associated Gospel Churches
Bible Church Movement
Christian and Missionary
  Alliance
Evangelical Covenant Church of
  America
Evangelical Free Church of
  America
Independent Fundamental
  Churches of America
Willow Creek Association

Friends Churches
Evangelical Friends International
Friends General Conference
  (Hicksites)
Religious Society of Friends

Holiness Churches
Brethren in Christ Church
Christian and Missionary Alliance
Christian Holiness Association
Church of God (Anderson,
  Indiana)
Church of the Nazarene
Salvation Army
United Holy Church of
  America
Wesleyan Church

**Inspirationist/Communal
Groups**
Amana Church Society
Doukhobors (Dukhobors)
Schwenkfelders (The

Schwenkfelder Church)
Shakers

Lutheran Churches
Evangelical Lutheran Church in
  America
Evangelical Lutheran Church in
  Canada
Lutheran Church—Missouri
  Synod
Wisconsin Evangelical Lutheran
  Synod

Mennonite Churches
See Anabaptist/Brethren/
  Mennonite Churches

Methodist Churches
African Methodist Episcopal
  Church
African Methodist Episcopal
  Zion Church
Christian Methodist Episcopal
  Church
Church of the United Brethren in
  Christ
Free Methodist Church of North
  America
United Methodist Church

Nonorthodox Groups
Church of Christ, Scientist
Church of Jesus Christ of
  Latter-day Saints (Mormons)
Church of the New Jerusalem
The Family
Jehovah's Witnesses
Liberal Catholic Church
Unification Church (Moonies)
Unitarian Univeralist
  Association
Unity School of Christianity

The Way, International

Orthodox Churches
See Eastern Orthodox Churches

Pentecostal Churches
Assemblies of God
Church of God (Cleveland,
  Tennessee)
Church of God in Christ
Church of God of Prophecy
International Church of the
  Foursquare Gospel
Pentecostal Church of Canada
United Pentecostal Church,
  International

**Presbyterian and Reformed
Churches**
Christian Reformed Church in
  North America
Conservative Congregational
  Christian Conference
Cumberland Presbyterian Church
Evangelical Presbyterian Church
General Synod of the Associate
  Reformed Presbyterian Church
Orthodox Presbyterian Church
Presbyterian Church in America
Presbyterian Church in Canada
Presbyterian Church (U.S.A.)
Reformed Church in America
Reformed Presbyterian Church
  in North America
United Church of Christ

Quaker Churches
See Friends Churches

Reformed Churches
See Presbyterian and Reformed
  Churches

Restorationist Churches
Christian Church (Disciples of
   Christ)
Church of Christ (Disciples of
   Christ) in Canada
Christian Churches/Churches of
   Christ (Independent)

Churches of Christ (Non-
   Instrumental)

Roman Catholic Church
Roman Catholic Church
See also Eastern-Rite Catholic
   Churches